Forever

Changed

Connie E. Schlepp
WEISKOPF

I am an Artist, Author and Minister of God's Word - a life changed through the power, love and grace of Jesus Christ. I share this gift of God to others through my art, writings and ministry. Whether I am speaking to a crowd of 500 or an audience of one.

To Purchase this book, art and other teachings, visit:
Connie Weiskopf Ministries at: www.cswmi.org
Or Via Mail:
P.O. Box 842
Firestone, Colorado 80520
Email: connie@cswmi.org

Cover art – watercolor "River of Light" by author & artist, Connie Schlepp Weiskopf – to view & purchase art, please visit www.cswmi.org

Unless otherwise noted, all scripture is from the King James Version. "KJV", Cambridge, 1769.

www.cswmi.org

Forever Changed

Connie E. Schlepp Weiskopf

Table of Contents

A Note from Connie:

Before beginning your journey try to remove all the 'religious' mindsets you may have and begin to read scripture with a mindset of His love and Grace.

Ephesians 1:15-20

Wherefore I also, after I heard of your faith in the Lord Jesus, and love unto all the saints, Cease not to give thanks for you, making mention of you in my prayers; ***That the God of our Lord Jesus Christ, the Father of*** ***glory, may give unto you the spirit of wisdom and*** ***revelation in*** *the knowledge of him: The eyes of your understanding being enlightened; that ye may know what is the hope of his calling, and what the riches of the glory of his inheritance in the saints, And what is the exceeding greatness of his power to us-ward who believe, according to the working of his mighty power, Which he wrought in Christ, when he raised him from the dead, and set him at his own right hand in the heavenly places.*

Foreword

Forever Changed is filled with powerful truths for all believers. Connie leads readers into the freedoms Christ bought for us and the fullness of life awaiting us here on earth. She reassures us that we can know our Father's voice and be confident in our relationship with Him. Her heart for all believers to walk in the abundance God has freely given us is evident throughout her writing.

Connie has lived and fought for the revelations she writes about. She has pressed into God and found treasures that she lovingly shares with her readers. Connie's words are sincere and direct and always supported by Scripture. She addresses common challenges to her viewpoint with grace and truth. Connie shares from personal experiences of standing on God's word and seeing God's faithfulness. After knowing Connie for the last few years, I can truly say she lives what she believes.

As I read Forever Changed, my spirit bubbled over with excitement and joy in the life Christ has invited me to live. I found my heart agreeing with her words of truth, and shouting Hallelujah over and over again. It changed my life.

This book is a must read for any believer who wants to walk deeper in the richness Christ has to offer. Get ready to be challenged, empowered and forever changed.

Karen Olson

Forever Changed
Introduction

My life is not one that would necessarily inspire others as you look at my flesh. But inside, put under a microscope you would see the DNA of Jesus Christ Himself.

When you examine yourself under a microscope does your life itself resemble that of Jesus Christ? Is it a desire deep in your heart that you would? Perhaps you have no desire to look like Jesus because of what you have been taught about Him. What if you were convinced that Jesus loves you and only wants the best for you. Not through sickness and disease, but through love and grace and life, filled with joy, health, peace, freedom and prosperity.

My desire the moment I gave my life to Christ was that I would resemble Him. I kept reading in His Word that I should be like Him and even greater, why didn't I? I must have a knowledge problem, maybe I wasn't born again, maybe I just had some unbelief. I began a journey to examine my life and the Life of Jesus Christ, and what it is I have now that I am a believer. I didn't want to go to the altar every Sunday to re-dedicate my life because I still didn't look like Him. I remember reading a saying back then and one that is still around "If you were arrested for being a Christian, would there be enough evidence to convict you?" Not too many of the people I knew had enough evidence of what God's Word said a Christian was. They went to Church, they even loved God. But besides that, they would have to let them go for lack of evidence.

I want to thank my incredible Savior for Sending His Son so that I might have life, and life abundant, the power of the Gospel, The Good News of Jesus Christ. I thank my husband David who has walked by my side as I searched for the truth in places I should not have. You stood by me when I finally said I found it and I want you to have it too. I thank my Pastors, Mike and Marilyn Miller of Fathers House in Ft. Collins, Colorado. Thank you for continuing to share the Truth. Andrew Wommack, for being bold and sharing the Good News of Jesus Christ and for making the scriptures become clear to me. Thank you Andrew for your prayers and being such a big part of my healing as well as Fathers House. Thank you to my good friends Cheryl, Karen and Colleen for helping edit. Lola, Lori and Linda who inspire me to be all that God has called me to be and to encourage me as I share the truth with those around me. I thank my family and the many volunteers and friends I have met at Life Choices who have been an encouragement and have seen Jesus in a way they may not have before. And have now begun to share Him with others, as they move out to other ministries and bring the 'Good News of Jesus Christ.' I love each of you more than you may imagine.

There is Power in the Gospel. I pray that each of you will take hold of 'The Truth' The Good News. When the Good News is preached, His Power is released. You need to take hold and believe and then receive it. You have the choice to accept or reject it. There is no middle ground, you either accept the finished work of Jesus at the cross or you don't!

I am forever changed because of the power of an incredible God who sent His Son, Jesus Christ.

"Let The Word of God get in the way of your religion."
(Andrew Wommack).

Chapter 1

Who Am I?

Who am I that the Son of God should shower me with His love and grace?

Who am I that I would be healed of cancer, prosperous, and set free from an old life of shame and guilt?

Who am I that I should be called righteous and holy?

Who am I?

I am nobody, but because of Jesus Christ and His sacrifice I am everything. I have it ALL. Without Him nothing, nada, zippo just plain old Connie, but with Him, everything. I am the new me, born again, filled with the Holy Spirit, living a life of joy, peace, health, patience, kindness, prosperity, forgiveness, goodness and self control! Or maybe I'm not so good, but my God says I am all these things and more because I believe! So, I am!

The chains of religion have been broken off and I am being set free, my life has been forever changed!

I desire that you would have it all and know and experience this incredible Jesus the way I have. Not just a good god, but an incredible God, that will change your life.

Who is He? Who is He that delivered me from death and a life of sickness? Who is He that created the universe and you and me with a spoken Word? Who is He that saved us all, that brings a peace beyond my own understanding and fills me with joy? If I could express to you one thing, it would be that God IS A GOOD GOD THAT LOVES YOU. He is not the God I grew up believing He was, ready to strike me with sickness, or punish me because I sinned. He loves me. He only wants the very best for me. I absolutely have to do nothing at all except believe that! Out of my love for Him and knowing His love for me, I desire to get to know Him and be the best that I can. Who Is He? He's the way to an incredible, filled life. He's a loving God who provided everything we need by sacrificing His Son for us all.

You are the way you are because of what you believe. What is it that you believe? I believed in Jesus, I just didn't know all He had nor did I know I had it all. I kept hearing and reading that I had the power of God to do mighty things. His power, not mine. He's given the life of His Son so that I could be doing the greater things He tells us in His Word. It's not about growing up or becoming like Christ but it's about coming into agreement of who I am and what I already have. If we never believe what the Bible of The Lord says we have, we will never have it! We are all complete In Him.

John 3:16 *For God so loved the world, that he gave his only begotten Son, that whosoever believeth in him should not perish, but have everlasting life.*

I grew up in a fairly large family. I was number five of six children. My parents were married very young and both came from large families. My upbringing was abusive in many ways and things happened that impacted my life in many negative ways. My heart changed. My mom would read to us from the Bible at night, I don't remember much of my childhood but I am so thankful that she laid a foundation that would bring me back to the arms of a loving Father, my LORD.

One event caused me to look at life through a different 'filter.' My boyfriend's best friend raped me at 16. This event caused me to have feelings of distrust and shame. The foundation of who Jesus was in my life, my perception of who He was made it so I didn't think He was someone I could turn to. All our behaviors are a reflection of who we 'perceive' ourselves to be. I was a sinner filled with the shame and guilt of a sinful lifestyle. That was what I was taught! I even put the blame on Him for the things that happened in my life, good and bad.

I made many bad choices as I looked for love in all the wrong places.

After college, I found myself in an abusive relationship with a man who stalked me, broke into my home and raped me at gun point on five separate occasions. I became pregnant and had my first abortion.

No one ever told me I had choices, only that abortion would solve my 'problem'. My baby was not the problem.

My guilt deepened as I tried to justify my actions. I tried to find a place for God in my life, but the God that I had been introduced to growing up would never be approachable as long as I had the internal guilt and shame.

In my woundedness I found myself in another unhealthy relationship with a man who was an alcoholic. His name was David.

David and I aborted our first child together and my heart truly died. I no longer felt, I only existed! This is a common side effect for women who have terminated a child.

I was invited to Church by my younger brother, and then again by my sister, who had given their lives to Christ. This time was different. I finally found a Church I wanted to become a part of, a place where I felt the love of the LORD. Actually, I began to fall madly and passionately in love with the LORD. But, once again I found myself pregnant. I thought if anyone knew I was pregnant they would know I was still living a life of sin and I would not be able to come and meet with this God I had just met. My religious upbringing, along with my life's experiences, had painted an abstract picture for me of who God was and in my skewed thinking I had only one answer. So I terminated my third child. As I lay on the table and waited for the procedure to begin, I wanted anyone, especially David to come in and say, "We can do this, we can bring this baby into the world, there is a way." but that didn't happen.

I soon gave my life to Christ though I believe I had done that the very first day I had fallen in love with Him, I just hadn't gone forward in the church and said any words aloud to confess that. I began to fall even more in love with Him and He began to work in my heart as I sought to know HIM, bringing healing. I wanted all that God had for me. He said I would be doing greater things than even He. "Raising the dead, healing the sick, opening blind eyes.

John 14:12-14 *Verily, verily, I say unto you, He that believeth on me, the works that I do shall he do also; and greater works than these shall he do; because I go unto my Father.*
And whatsoever ye shall ask in my name, that will I do, that the Father may be glorified in the Son. If ye shall ask any thing in my name, I will do it.

Matthew 10:8 *Heal the sick, cleanse the lepers, raise the dead, cast out devils: freely ye have received, freely give.*

The LORD became everything I had been searching for. He became my best friend, and my husband. As my best friend I learned to know His voice.

The first day after I gave my life to Christ I told David we could no longer have sex. The next day I told him he had to move out. He agreed and we tried to make our relationship work but my passions had already been changing for Christ.

My hearts desire was to let others know about this Jesus that I had fallen in love with. I wanted others to know His forgiveness, love, grace and healing. I wanted everyone to be doing the greater things He said we would be doing. I wanted to be doing them! I just didn't have the knowledge of who He was yet and what I could do, because of what He did!

David and I separated. After two years had passed God told me I was to be David's wife. My first reaction was to tell God He must mean another David. He would not call me to marry the David I knew after being single 42 years. Besides, God was my husband. God asked me to pray for David. I told God "I'll pray for the man, but I will not marry him." God began to once again change my heart as I spent time with Him. I began to wake up two times a night to pray for David, not because I wanted to. God delivered David miraculously from his addictions.

So here we are, married. I left Colorado and moved to Utah where David was living and working at the time. Before moving to Utah, I studied much in Bible College about the local culture there. Utah is predominately Mormon. God's words to me were to love them as He does.

I had visited a Baptist Church when God called me to go to Utah the first time to see David. There are not as many options in the state other than the Mormon Church. When we were married this is the one we decided best fit our beliefs. It was more of a non-denominational Church and we fell in love with the people who were in leadership and the congregation.

A friend who was the head of the women's ministry at our Church invited us to a banquet for a ministry where she was on the board. The ministry was for a pregnancy center. I had never even heard of a pregnancy center before: David and I were just going to support our friend.

When one of the speakers began to share her story, it was everything I could do not to fall to the floor and begin to cry. However, seated at the table with us that night was the 'head of women's ministry' from our Church, the Pastor and his wife and the associate pastor and his wife. My shame and guilt would not allow me to let them know that I too had had abortions. I never wanted anyone to know. David and I had never talked about our abortions and I had never told him about my first one. When the banquet let out, we went to the car and I began to weep. My husband looked at me, grabbed my hand and said, "You know God has forgiven us, don't you?" I cried and said, "I don't know that." We talked more, and I began to have an interest in knowing more about this pregnancy center and how to get involved.

Fundraising banquets have a special meaning to me; it was at a banquet that healing began to manifest in my husband and me. For the first time we began to openly talk about our choices to terminate our children and we began to let God's healing pour into our hearts. God says, "The truth sets you free." We let the truth come out and Gods healing in.

Once again I realized how much I wanted to give back by sharing my story and truth with other young girls who found themselves in an unplanned pregnancy. I never wanted another girl or young man to believe the lies I had been told. I was told, it was just a blob of tissue and that abortion would solve my problem. Abortion did not solve my problem, actually it added about ten more. I was approximately seven and a half weeks pregnant with one of those pregnancies. Your baby has a heart beat at three weeks and has brain waves and fingers and toes and every organ at five and a half. I wanted them to know there is help and hope for them and that there is a precious life after pregnancy no matter the outcome.

David and I moved back to Colorado. We attended a concert at a local Church. At the end was an invitation to give to Life Choices pregnancy center. The Executive Director at the time spoke and I quietly said to myself I'd like to get involved with the center. I really thought that there was only one pregnancy center in the world and that was in Ogden, Utah. I was surprised to find out that there were two of them, and God had moved me to a city where it was. I chuckle now as I have discovered, there are pregnancy centers in many of the major cities and urban areas across America. I didn't know! One day I stopped in at Life Choices and asked if they needed any volunteers. I began the next week.

Most pregnancy centers offer healing for post abortion. I thought I had finished the majority of my healing from my own abortions. I had attended Bible College, received counseling, spent hours with the Father as He showed me the bitterness in my heart and helped set me free from much of my past. I signed up for the Bible study class. It was called Forgiven and Set Free. If there was more that God wanted to give my life, I sought it from Him.

Matthew 7:7 *Ask, and it shall be given you; seek, and ye shall find; knock, and it shall be opened unto you:*

Jeremiah 29:13 *And ye shall seek me, and find me, when ye shall search for me with all your heart.*

God is so wonderful and faithful that He cares about every detail of our lives. He went to the deepest pain in my heart and in this class set me free from the things I didn't know were still there.

One of the things He showed me was that I still carried unforgiveness in my heart for the people involved in my abortions. I needed to forgive the doctors and nurses who provided the procedure without giving me the information, David for not standing by me and myself for involving them in my abortions and going through with the abortions. I cried tears in the class that cleansed a heart filled with pain, shame and guilt.

In the class we named all our babies and for the first time I saw that I am a mom even though I terminated the only children I would ever conceive. I also now have been blessed with a step son through my marriage to David. I named my first child Isaiah Thomas. David and I named our children Jordan Elizabeth, and Isaac David. We placed a plaque at the tomb for the unborn in Boulder, Colorado. David did not attend the ceremony we had at the wall. I see that he is still struggling at times with the choices we made and I pray that he is set free as I was from any shame and quilt. The day the class went to the wall, our plaques were already placed, we had a service with a local pastor there to pray. The class released balloons, as we watched them rise and fade out of sight. I knew my children were now in the arms of a loving Father in Heaven and I was able to grieve the loss of my children. No matter how they were lost.

I find women who have terminated a child feel as though they are not allowed or have no right to grieve that loss, because it was a choice they had made. I pray that they would find a pregnancy center in the city they live and begin their healing journey.

God does care about every detail of our lives. He wants us set free from everything that would keep us from the life of freedom in HIM.

I had been dissatisfied in Church, because I was not seeing God's manifestation of the healings and freedoms He said we should be experiencing as believers in Him. I began to search in many of the different Church's available in Colorado. I was attending a Torah Study, thinking they might have the more and the greater things God said we would be doing as His children. (Matthew 10:8 – Heal the sick, cleanse the lepers, raise the dead, cast out devils: freely ye have received, freely give.)

God spoke to me one day after asking for some prayer for healing. "Connie, You do not even believe Me to forgive you all your sins, how will you believe Me for your healing?" This moved me to tears, and I said to God, "But God, I have committed so many sins, how can You forgive all that?" He spoke again and said "Then I sent My Son for nothing!"

This deeply moved me, and I began to see my disbelief fade and the faith within me rise to new levels with understanding, freedom and power I had never known.

I truly was becoming the over comer I would read about in scripture.

1 John 5:4 *For whatsoever is born of God overcometh the world: and this is the victory that overcometh the world, even our faith.*

1 John 5:5 *Who is he that overcometh the world, but he that believeth that Jesus is the Son of God?*

God asked me leave the Torah study I had been attending. Not because it was bad. I found great friendships there and learned many wonderful things in the Old Testament, Torah study. He told me I was going back to the law, and said, "I have done away with the law." That was one of the main reasons He had sent His Son. I heard His words again, "Then I sent My Son for nothing." After this experience with the LORD, I studied everything in the Bible about healing and what it was that Jesus truly accomplished when He sacrificed His life for us at the cross. I studied every Word on receiving and began this incredible journey that I am still on today.

I was diagnosed with breast cancer shortly after becoming involved at Life Choices. Breast cancer is another statistic for women who have terminated a child. Your risks increase each time you make the choice of abortion. But God was showing me about His healing and I am not a statistic in the eyes of our LORD. James 5:14-15 says "If anyone is sick to go to the elders, have them lay hands on you and anoint you and pray, and the prayer offered up in faith will heal the sick. So I sought His healing through His Word and began learning about His grace. I still had many wrong beliefs about who God was, who I was. I worked hard to know what HE said about me, my health, and my life and to renew my mind to all HIS TRUTHS.

I learned there is more that we are to be doing in the Church and I had been looking for it to manifest. God is the One who said we the Church would do more than Jesus did while on the earth, healing the sick and raising the dead.

Mark 16:17 *And these signs shall follow them that believe; In my name shall they cast out devils; they shall speak with new tongues; They shall take up serpents; and if they drink any deadly thing, it shall not hurt them; they shall lay hands on the sick, and they shall recover.*

So I looked for someone who believed in all that God has provided for each of us who believe. I looked for someone that when they prayed people were healed. I contacted Andrew Wommack Ministries by e-mail asking if Andrew could come and pray for me. They nicely replied that he was very busy and could not do that. I e-mailed them back saying I would pay him! They once again replied and said he would be ministering at a Church in Colorado Springs and if I would come early, he would probably pray for me. I did just that and spent a few days in Colorado Springs reading the Word and having some fun conversations with my Lord. I remember the message Andrew gave was about the balance of grace and faith. It was exactly what I needed to hear to receive my healing. Andrew asked me if I was ready to receive my healing. He then said a simple prayer, agreeing with me and commanding the cancer to leave my body and not return. I also went for prayer and was anointed with oil at the healing rooms at my Church. Andrew asked me that day he prayed for me if I was in a Church that believed in the healing power of God and that was teaching truth. I had just visited Father's House in Ft. Collins and this was the Church Andrew suggested I attend.

I didn't believe enough or have the full understanding of my healing at this time to not go in for the surgery. I had the biopsy weeks prior to my meeting with Andrew and the Drs. Diagnosis was not what I had wanted to hear. It used to bring fear when I heard the word cancer. I spent some time with the LORD to overcome any fear the doctors, friends or the reports of others planted in my mind. I continually read the Word of God and His truths to overcome their words and replace them with the truth of who God said I was. "By His stripes I am healed." I had many scriptures I wrote down to counter the lies and words of others.

The day after my breast cancer surgery the doctor called and said, "We don't know what happened, there was no more cancer to be found." I said, "I know what happened. God healed me" David and I praised God and rejoiced in HIM. The journey I took to understand and receive God's healing began much earlier, with much diligence. I will be sharing more of this journey with you in the following chapters. I have never had any more treatment of any kind, no chemo, no radiation or drugs. Even though the doctors advised me to do 'something.' My reply to their suggestions is that if God healed me why would I need anything else.

Statistics reveal that by tomorrow morning over 6,000 lives will be taken by abortion. The hearts of 12,000 will be changed, affecting the lives, families and communities around them. Over 51 million lives have been affected in America alone. This Sunday if you attend Church, look around you. Over 40% of the women will have experienced an abortion in their lives.

Of the women who terminate a child, 75% say they are believers or Christians when they make this choice. These statistics are starting to change as we begin to share the truth about abortion and the sanctity of life.

I want to share with everyone I meet the character and forgiveness of Jesus Christ and how He reveals Himself in His Word bringing hope, healing, grace, love and the restoration each individual needs.

I love the movie 'Schindler's List.' At the end of that movie we see Schindler looking at a gold ring on his finger with tears in his eyes saying, that this gold could have brought enough money to me to save another life. Or two or three. I relate it to the pregnancy center ministry. More lives are lost to abortion than in the Holocaust. My heart says "let's educate one more young girl, one more child LORD, about the love, healing and forgiveness of Our LORD Jesus Christ." I want everyone to know His love and all that they have available to them because of Jesus Christ and what He did at the cross. He paid the price for us by sacrificing His life for ours. Abortion will not solve your problem. Your baby is not the problem.

The Lord called me out of my 25 years of self-employment as an artist to the position of Life Choices

Center Director in 2007.

I get to share the truth so that women know they can make a choice for life. I share that there is a loving gracious God who took care of all of our sins at the cross. He either did it all, or nothing at all. I get to share the power of Jesus Christ, which is available to those who believe. I have witnessed many healings from emotional to physical including cancers, arthritis, hepatitis C, shoulder and knee injuries and many other healings.

The greatest joy I receive is when salvations occur and I see others getting It, getting to know about this incredible love of a good God. Most of the people I see and meet think God is the One who brings tragedy and sickness and afflictions to teach us life lessons. I also see many who, because of the circumstances in their lives feel upset if I pray for them and then Thank God for their healing. If you are in need of healing and don't believe you are good enough or have prayed hard enough or deserve all He has, keep reading. My desire is that you live a life of victory over every affliction, over every emotional upset and anything else this world, the enemy of our own thoughts might have, that keep us from living the abundant, overflowing wonderful life of Christ.

Matthew 25:21 *His lord said unto him, Well done, thou good and faithful servant: thou hast been faithful over a few things, I will make thee ruler over many things: enter thou into the joy of thy lord.*

Luke 7:47-50 summed up says, *"Those forgiven much, love much"*

Lord, thank you for your forgiveness and your incredible love. There is One who redeems, One who has already done it all for those He loves, His name is Jesus Christ.

Chapter 2

Planting the Seeds of a Strong Foundation

God's answer to the pain and suffering of this present world is Jesus Christ. Jesus is His evidence of God's incredible love for man.

John 3:16 *For God so loved the world, that he gave his only begotten Son, that whosoever believeth in him should not perish, but have everlasting life.*

BE CONVINCED!

When we come to know and believe in Jesus Christ and we give our lives to Him, we now have a new foundation. Most of us are still living in the past with the foundation of our old lives, believing that we are only products of our upbringing and of our 'natural' mother and father. We are not believing in the finished work of Jesus Christ. So are we truly born again? I now have a new life in Christ. I have my awesome family, but Jesus is written in my DNA, my DNA is now the same as His. I have His blood surging through me. I no longer am a product of the past but of the new life in Christ.

He says in, 2 Cor. 5:17 *"If any man be In Christ, he is a new creature, old things are passed away behold all things are become new"*

And in, Ephesians 4:24 He says, *"And that ye put on the new man which is created in righteousness and true holiness"*.

Now I am not Holy or righteous, but because of my new life in Christ, I am created righteous and holy. Most people read this in the scriptures but are still told they must 'work' their way to this new life in Christ, to holiness and right-standing. I do agree that there is some work to be done, but it does not mean that if you are not serving in missions, standing on a street corner, praying two hours a day or giving your time to the Church, you will not have a good foundation. Your foundation is found and formed by reading the Word, spending time in the Word and looking to and believing Jesus, Our LORD. Your new life in Christ is about having an intimate relationship with the One who created you, loves you and died for you. It's about Him and everything He did, it has nothing to do with anything we do, except believe. But to believe, I need to know Him.

If we do not know what we have we will continue to live our lives in the old ways, believing the old lies the enemy has told us about our selves. We need a new foundation. Well, we already have it, most of us just don't know it!

When we give our lives to Christ (born again) no matter if it is in front of the Church or on our bedroom floor, we come just as we are, with all our sins, guilt, shame, and insecurities. These things do not immediately go away, though many eventually do. For instance, when I gave my life to Christ, the words I spoke changed almost overnight. I no longer could say the "F" word, which used to flow quickly from my tongue. Taking my God's name in vain slipped a few times, but actually made me sad. I just didn't want to continue speaking as I once did. It was not because I thought I would no longer have a relationship with My Jesus, but just because He loved me so much and I Him.

The first day after I gave my life to Christ I told my then boyfriend David that we could not longer have sex. The following day I asked him to move out. He agreed. We tried to make our relationship work, but again, I had now fallen madly in love with Jesus, and my thoughts were now on Him.

Other things in our lives take time to change like smoking. It was several months after I gave my life to Him that I was standing in the shower one morning and the Lord spoke clearly to me "Connie, if you don't have that first cigarette, I will take it from you", I made it a few hours, and then I had a cigarette. This same thing happened the next day with me lighting up another cigarette. On the third morning the Lord gently spoke the same words. This time my reply was, "If you are going to tell me three mornings and give me three chances, I am not going to have another cigarette." I never craved another cigarette and to this day really hate the smell of them. God is so patient with us. He will meet us where we are. I didn't know that I had so much given to me from God at that time, but knew that I wanted all that God said we would have. "Where is it LORD?" I wasn't seeing it in the Church at the time. When we give our lives to Christ, we are accepted in the Church just as we are, but soon find out that if certain things do not change, we are told things like;

"What sin are you not confessing?"

"What sin are you committing?"

"What curses are you accepting?"

"You must be doing something wrong."

Perhaps a few of these questions stated were true. God saved me the way I was yesterday, but now I'm being told I have to do something to prove that and then I will be healed, forgiven, prosperous and set free. No! Once I was saved, it was a done deal. Jesus did it all at the cross. He said, "It is finished" (John 19:30) The only thing I need to do is really believe that it is done.

I began to change my foundation and renew my mind to the truth of God and what He says about me. I needed a true revelation of who God was in my life and who I was in Him. I needed to begin to plant the seeds of His truth in me. God's Word is the seed. The process of seed, time, and harvest is unchangeable. We must first plant a seed, and then there is a time of watering and the sunshine giving life. We watch the seed grow and finally we can harvest. If we never plant a seed of corn, we will never get corn. If we never plant a seed of truth there is nothing to harvest. God also began to caution and show me that we can plant unbelief and wrong things (seeds) by listening to wrong teachings and by feeding ourselves all the "unbeliefs" that are out there. I began to read the Word every chance I could. I went to every Church service, went to Bible College and fed and planted as much as possible. I wanted all God had for me and I knew the only place to find it would be in His Word. My family thought I was a 'Jesus Freak' and had really gone off the deep end. I was not willing to live the 'marginal' Christian life anymore. I will still go to heaven. He tells me there is heaven on earth, right now, and I was looking for that. I knew it was here. He said it in His Word. He is not a liar. I knew others desperately needed it too - they were dying. They didn't have a revelation of His truths.

I read and was told that we would be doing even greater things than He but I wasn't seeing the things He did do being repeated by Christians, let alone the greater things. I knew my God did and does not lie. Maybe I misunderstood the Word. "No," that wasn't it, I was determined. I read and believed everything He says. I don't interpret it through traditions and religion. Some traditions may be ok but many make the Word of God of no effect.

Mark 7:13 *Making the word of God of none effect through your tradition, which ye have delivered: and many such like things do ye.*

I didn't know where else to go. I began to read and search other books for more truth. I knew in my spirit that a lot of what I read was tainted with man's understanding or lack of understanding and wisdom. As I shared in the previous chapter I thought maybe the Jewish Church had the answers for me. I attended a 'Messianic Jewish congregation.' I still didn't see the signs and wonders and the greater things God said we would have. I did love the dancing and worship, and still do. I love dancing before my Jesus, and with my Jesus. Some of my favorite times are with music, when I get to just praise my precious Lord. I love songs that are focused entirely on Him and praising Him. I recognize them so clearly now, where before they were pretty songs. There are some wonderful songs by Christian artists, I just change the words when I sing them to line up with His truths. Many of the beautiful songs I learned in Church or heard really spoke unbelief to me and lacked the truth of who Jesus really is and who I am in Him. Many songs were calling Jesus to "come on down!" He's already here!

I met some incredible friends in the Messianic Church who are searching for "the more" and believe this is where it is. It was also the loss a friend's baby that helped me to look further. We so believed that God was going to heal their child that we prayed and believed for his healing to take place. We believed for God to heal him and when he died we believed God would raise him from the dead. When that didn't happen my foundation was moved once again. This was when God told me to leave the Messianic Church and told me that I had 'returned to the law.' "But isn't the law good, Lord?" I asked, the Lord responded. "I demolished the law and wrote the law in your heart when I gave my one and only son to die on the cross for you". It was on one of my last visits to the Torah study that the Lord spoke and said "Connie, you do not even believe that I have forgiven you your sins, how will you believe me for your healing?" I wept a lot that day when I got home and that's when I began getting into His Word even more and studying all I could about our awesome God.

I began to study everything in His Word on believing and receiving and what it actually was that Jesus did for us at the cross. He sent His Son and saved us. The word Saved in the New Testament is the word SOZO in Hebrew, which means, healed, forgiven, prosperous, and set free.

2 Timothy 1:9 *Who hath saved us, and called us with an holy calling, not according to our works, but according to his own purpose and grace, which was given us in Christ Jesus before the world began.*

Saved does not mean I just get to go to heaven when I die. Though if that was all I got, that is wonderful. I also studied every scripture on being saved, on healing, forgiveness, prosperity and on being set free. Wow, what an incredible journey, what an incredible foundation the Lord has given to me (to us) as believers in Jesus Christ. I just didn't know or understand it before. "The truth sets you free." However, if you don't know that, it can't. Read the Word and believe it. "It's the truth YOU KNOW that sets you free." Study the Word so that you can KNOW who He is. Do not settle. Find out what His promises are to us and then believe.

Begin to lay that new foundation. Begin to believe the foundation you have and not in what others tell you that you have, or what you have learned in Sunday school. Andrew Wommack has said "Let the Word of God get in the way of what you believe or of your religion."

The seed, time, and harvest makes up one of God's laws that are still in effect. Plant the Word and water it with the Word, then you will see a harvest in your life. Many people plant a seed, but either don't take the time to feed on the Word, or they dig up the seed before it is time. Then they think there is nothing to this healing, it's not working. It's already been done, but for it to manifest you have to do your part. Your part is to believe.

Many are waiting for God to do what He told us to do. He tells us to heal the sick, raise the dead.

I am guilty of the same. I asked God to heal my friend's baby. What I learned later is that He asked me to do that. I didn't know at the time. I was asking God to do what He told me to do. I needed to lay hands on that baby and command his little body to be healed.

James 5:14-15 *Is any sick among you? let him call for the elders of the church; and let them pray over him, anointing him with oil in the name of the Lord: And the prayer of faith shall save the sick, and the Lord shall raise him up; and if he have committed sins, they shall be forgiven him.*

If anyone is sick, Go to the elders. That is what God is waiting for us to do and what He told us to do. I am an elder, I have the same raising from the dead power living on the inside of me, but when I was still feeding my belief, I went to the elders, I went to those whom I saw opening blind eyes, not the ones who had no fruit when they prayed.

Speak to the mountains. What is your mountain? Are sicknesses, finances, emotions, addictions, your mountain? Begin to plant the seed of truth in you and keep standing on God's Word. Do not pull up the seed before its time. If the healing doesn't manifest the moment you tell it to, keep standing on the truth. Water the Word and stand on God's Truth until you see it manifest. Do not abort the miracle before it happens. Conception cannot take place without first planting a seed, then we get to see the fruit, the miracle! Remember, we never get to see the miracle, the signs and wonders if we abort the miracle (seed) before it is harvested, before it is complete.

I have now worked in a pregnancy center for several years, and see women aborting their children before those babies are ever given a chance. I did the same. I listened to a lie that Satan and the world fed me and I didn't trust in the finished work of Jesus. I never took the time to see. To see that my baby had fingers and toes and was living. I had a knowledge problem. Our miracles need time. Sometimes that time can be 3 seconds, or 3 minutes or three weeks but I do not believe it should ever be two years, or three or more. I never saw the miracles take that much time in the Word. Three weeks was the longest we see in the Word for a miracle to manifest. The only reason it took that long was because of unbelief. He already had it before he asked.

We need to stand on the truth; so that when we do not see the manifestation of our healing, prosperity, or mountain moved, we do not abort the miracle. God tells us to keep standing.

Ephesians 6:11 *Put on the whole armor of God, that ye may be able to stand against the wiles of the devil.*

If all we did was rely on what we see, we would most likely abort many miracles before they have taken place. I have entertained the lies of well meaning friends and Christians and aborted many miracles that would have taken place in my life. NO MORE! I am praying that the wisdom and knowledge that God is providing through His Word will not allow me to go back to the way I once was. I pray that if I ever entertain that place again, my Jesus will quicken me to look at Him and not at the things of this world. We have a new set of 'laws' as believers that unbelievers do not get to take advantage of simply because they do not believe. We all get to take advantage of the law of gravity. But how many take hold of the 'law of healing?' God already provided this for everyone of us non believers as well. He did it all at the cross. He provided all we need. He has already finished everything that He is going to do for us. Now it is up to us to believe and receive the finished work - His finished work. If you do not believe, you cannot receive.

How do you lay this foundation of His?

1. First you need to believe in Him, In Jesus Christ the Son of God. It is not about saying a few words, like I was told to say by someone, but to actually BELIEVE. Though this may sound simple, it does go a little deeper and there are many forms of belief or perhaps there are just many forms of unbelief .

Do you truly believe that God sent His Son? Do you believe that Jesus died on the cross for us and for our salvation?

Salvation = saved = SOZO = healed, forgiven, prosperous, set-free.

Because of His sacrifice I truly am healed? I truly am prosperous, forgiven healed and set free. Set free from all my sins, past, present and future! Set free from a past that was filled with ugliness and darkness and now I am living in the glorious light of a loving and gracious Father. Do I really understand His love? Most of us come with an understanding that was thrown at us by a dysfunctional family not really understanding His kind of love and how very much He loves us. It's not so much about our love for Him, though I can say I am still madly 'in love' with the Father, the Son and Holy Spirit'. Do you understand His love for you?

2. Begin to renew your mind to His 'truths.' Plant the seeds of truth in you by reading The Word, by asking Him to reveal His truths to you as you read. Starve your unbelief and feed your belief.

3. Don't dig up the seed you plant before the proper time. His time has been given to read the Word and feed those seeds you planted. The time provided is how we produce in our lives. Time belongs to me, not sickness or disease,

not even the economy. We must choose 'good' seed.

Leviticus 19:19b........*thou shalt not sow thy field with mingled seed:* .... What seeds have you received in your heart? Life or death? Even a little unbelief cancels out the truth.

1 Corinthians 5:6 *Your glorying is not good. Know ye not that a little leaven leaveneth the whole lump?*

1 Peter 1:23 *Being born again, not of corruptible seed, but of incorruptible, by the word of God, which liveth and abideth for ever.*

God intended time to be our Grace and blessing.

Psalm 39:7 *And now, Lord, what wait I for? my hope is in thee.*

We already have everything in us, the time is for us to renew our minds to the truth to receive and harvest the fruit.

4. Believe! Be convinced!

Psalm 71:5 *For thou art my hope, O Lord God: thou art my trust from my youth.*

Jesus has already healed you. If you're convinced you need to wait on God to heal you, you will never see the healing manifest. It's wrong thinking, He tells us it's already done.

5. You cannot stand on someone else's foundation or build your own house on theirs. You must build your own foundation. Plant your own field, water, nurture and harvest it. This doesn't mean you cannot learn from others (especially me). You need a revelation understanding for yourself.

Ephesians 1:15-17 *Wherefore I also, after I heard of your faith in the Lord Jesus, and love unto all the saints, Cease not to give thanks for you, making mention of you in my prayers; That the God of our Lord Jesus Christ, the Father of glory, may give unto you the spirit of wisdom and revelation in the knowledge of him:*

I read many books and study guides by other teachers. I researched them to see if there was fruit and truth in their lives. Andrew Wommack has many wonderful teaching articles, books, CD's and tapes that are great teaching tools. John G. Lake, Smith Wigglesworth, Mike Miller from Fathers House in Ft. Collins Colorado. I searched for a place that I would not be fed unbelief anymore. Not that all Churches are bad, I just needed the 'more' the greater things of Jesus. I no longer wanted to settle and sit under the teachings of 'partial truths' or unbelief. Those partial truths were killing me.

6. Begin to do as He has asked us to do. Heal the sick, raise the dead, open blind eyes. You need to begin to walk it out, and do as He has asked. You cannot hide in a 'prayer closet' and expect God to do what He told us to! Don't give up. If you do not see the manifestations happen right away it does not mean that they will not manifest in an hour or week. But keep on standing and doing as He has asked of us. Don't abort the miracle. Expect them now, because it's already been provided for.

John 14:12 *Verily, verily, I say unto you, He that believeth on me, the works that I do shall he do also; and greater works than these shall he do; because I go unto my Father.*

I don't think most of us are so confident when we begin to do these things upon salvation. I don't think most of us are even 100% successful and have every person healed, delivered, prospered, and set-free when we do begin to minister the truth and pray for them. But the numbers begin to increase the more and more you see the manifestation of His truths come when you pray. Our confidence (BELIEF) grows and when we pray we will pray believing and not hoping (wishful thinking). I no longer pray just 'hoping' anymore but 'nearly' always pray believing. I am often surprised when the manifestation does not take place within at least a week. I can often tell who is ready to receive their healing, so I will share the truth with them and pray for them to receive His truths so they can receive His healing. When I do not see the manifestation in my own life, I will ask the Lord to reveal to me the un-belief. "Where is the un-belief Father?" "Help me in my unbelief."

Mark 9:24 *And straightway the father of the child cried out, and said with tears, Lord, I believe; help thou mine unbelief.* We can walk in both belief and unbelief at the same time. Believing some things yet experiencing unbelief in other areas of our lives.

It is never ME doing the healing, though God uses me and willing vessels. People who are willing to fail for God and for others sake, often suffer the persecutions that are in this world and in the Church, But God never fails. When I stand up for God's truth about healing and pray for the sick, I am often ridiculed and told those things are not for today. I simply ask if they want to know God's truth and point them to the scriptures that reveal these truths. It is their choice to believe or not.

For those who dare to be doing the more, there is persecution. It's okay. God provided the healing 2000 years ago with the sacrifice of His Son. He more than provided, He put Healing into every single one of us. Now He has given me the power and authority to use that gift to touch the lives of others.

Believe it and receive it.

God's Love and Grace

I cannot talk about laying a foundation without getting to the place where I know about His kind of Love and Grace. I briefly touched on it, but you need to leave your old ideas behind about what love is and let Him reveal to you and show you His love. He is not the kind of Father that wants to harm or hurt you in any way. He only wants to bless you and love you and show you His grace whenever 'we' feel like we have fallen short. When I came to know Jesus I began to 'know' that my way of thinking was not in line with what God was telling me in His Word. "God help me to know? Help to change my thinking!" As I spent time with Him He began to give me a clearer understanding of His love. I remember looking in the mirror one day and seeing myself through His eyes for the first time. I no longer saw an ugly chubby girl. I really was far from that. But because words had been spoken into my life, I saw myself as chubby. I weighed about 95 pounds at the time. I even began to see others differently and began to see colors as more vibrant and beautiful. As an artist, it was incredible to me. I still see colors in this new light of their own beauty. I have heaven right here on earth. I get it all now.

God began to reveal the depth of His love for me, me, Connie and He can do the same for you. He sent His one and only Son to come to earth. He came to earth as a man to suffer, to die for me, for you, to wage and fight a victorious fight against the enemy once and for all, for all of us. He took all my sins, sickness and ugliness upon Himself at the cross, all of it. I have enough sins of my own that He suffered for, but He actually took on every sin of every person for evermore. That is one reason I believe He was unidentifiable as a man on the cross. Not only because of the beating He took, but because of the sins He took from us all. Would you do that? Would you die for my sins? Send your only Son to die for my sins? NOT. And thankfully, He already did this and finished it at the cross and will not ever ask this of us. Praise God!

His love is so incredibly deep. He is there in every situation that you 'put' yourself in, to be there for you, and with you.

One truth that seems to be lost in the Church, and with believers, is His will for our lives. What is God's will for us? First of all He says; "above all else I wish that you would prosper and be in good health"

3 John 1:2 *Beloved, I wish above all things that thou mayest prosper and be in health, even as thy soul prospereth.*

His will for us is never to cause us harm or leave us without provision. To give us sickness, diseases or accidents. He went about healing all who were sick who believed. Matthew 9:35 *And Jesus went about all the cities and villages, teaching in their synagogues, and preaching the gospel of the kingdom, and healing every sickness and every disease among the people.*

He has left with us the power and authority to do the things He said, "Heal the sick, raise the dead, open blind eyes, make the lame to walk. " Not to let them suffer and die. The pat answer to those who haven't seen their healing transpire seems to be, "Well, God sometimes says "No." Why would this awesome God say no to you and yes to me. I am not any better, and I am probably worse than you. Why would He do that? He says His answer is always "Yes and Amen" to those who believe.

2 Corinthians 1:20 *For all the promises of God in him are yea, and in him Amen, unto the glory of God by us.*

Look at His Word and what He says is in His will. Is it to never work and have your pocket filled with cash. He says His will is that we should prosper. But you cannot just do nothing to achieve that prosperity. God cannot bless welfare or a person who is unwilling to work at all. He can bless those who are using their hands at something. You can't prosper nothing!

1 Thessalonians 4:11 *And that ye study to be quiet, and to do your own business, and to work with your own hands, as we commanded you; faith without works is dead.*

James 2:26 *For as the body without the spirit is dead, so faith without works is dead also.*

Again. He cannot do anything that is outside of His will for our lives. He is not going to change gravity because I just jumped off that bridge. He has set certain things into law. "The law of gravity." "The law of healing and prosperity."

There are many reasons people do not receive healing or prosperity. Believing or unbelief! But there are many factors to believing. God says many times for us to just believe.

1 John 5:5 *Who is he that overcometh the world, but he that believeth that Jesus is the Son of God?*

1 John 3:23 *And this is his commandment, That we should believe on the name of his Son Jesus Christ, and love one another, as he gave us commandment.*

How do we get to the place of believing? I can tell you that you will not get there by watching every TV show and then reading the word two minutes a day or week, or by listening and reading every negative thing in this world. You need to feed that belief. You need to be in the Word, reading, studying, feeding on the Truth.

But How do I know what the truth is? Isn't God's Word up to the interpretation of the person reading it? I absolutely disagree with those statements. For if you are really in The Word, studying and searching the scriptures, studying the meaning of the words Our Lord spoke, I believe there is little left to the vain imaginations and interpretation of the reader. Our Lord is pretty clear. He says what He means and He means what He says. Yes He talks in Parables at time. But if you read the before and after, it is still very clear what He is talking about. I have heard Christians say God's Word contradicts itself.

I have never come across someone who says that this has been in The Word on a regular basis and studies His Word. The contradiction that I have heard people say, is in the 'Gospels.' After studying Gods Word for some time now, I see that we have different men writing to different groups of people about the same story throughout the Gospels. Is it not true that you may tell the exact same story to 3 different people and because of 'their' particular background, gender, etc., you may emphasize different parts of the story, or you may even leave some parts out when sharing with certain people. This is the same with the Gospels. If you read the stories you will see they are the same.

It is usually those who spend no time building a relationship with Our Lord but only listening to a pastor here or there on TV, or on Sunday for twenty minutes who are confused about the Word of God. And I say usually because there are other factors that can come into play with someone's belief. How did you grow up? What Church were you in?

It is by the Word of God that we overcome. Choose to be a thankful receiver.

Prayer: Thank you Lord that Your Word is the seed in my life that I will not pull up before it's time.

2 Timothy 2:15 *Study to shew thyself approved unto God, a workman that needeth not to be ashamed, rightly dividing the word of truth.*

Hebrews 4:12 *For the word of God is quick, and powerful, and sharper than any twoedged sword, piercing even to the dividing asunder of soul and spirit, and of the joints and marrow, and is a discerner of the thoughts and intents of the heart.*

Romans 10:17 *So then faith cometh by hearing, and hearing by the word of God.*

Ephesians 5:6 *Let no man deceive you with vain words: for because of these things cometh the wrath of God upon the children of disobedience*

Gods Will:

3 John 1:2 *I wish above all else that you would prosper and be in good health.*

Galatians 1:4 *Who gave himself for our sins, that he might deliver us from this present evil world, according to the will of God and our Father:*

1 Thessalonians 5:18 *In every thing give thanks: for this is the will of God in Christ Jesus concerning you.*

Hebrews 2:4 *God also bearing them witness, both with signs and wonders, and with divers miracles, and gifts of the Holy Ghost, according to his own will?*

Hebrews 8:10 *For this is the covenant that I will make with the house of Israel after those days, saith the Lord; I will put my laws into their mind, and write them in their hearts: and I will be to them a God, and they shall be to me a people:*

1 Peter 2:15 *For so is the will of God, that with well doing ye may put to silence the ignorance of foolish men:*

Chapter 3

How to Hear the Voice of God

"How do you know that was God speaking to you in the car? How do you know it wasn't just your own thoughts, voice, or even Satan?

When your mother calls you on the phone, do you almost always know it's her? When your best friend calls do you recognize his or her voice? I have a built in 'caller ID' that tells me it's God! We spend so much time with our parents and best friend(s), that unless they are intentionally disguising their voice when they call, we nearly always know who it is. Unless of course there's a bad signal. It is the same with my God, or "my Daddy," as I call Him. I spent years with The Lord, getting to know Him, spending time in His Word, listening to His voice and still do. When He speaks to me, I almost always recognize Him. There have been moments when I used to ask. "Is that you Daddy?" If I really question that signal, I can always check what He has spoken or what I have heard with His Word. Does it line up with what He says? Because of the things we have learned in Church or through the world, our reception could be filled with some static that distorts the reception or our perception of what God meant.

I spend all day with my Daddy (God) getting to know His character, His true character. Not what I heard from the pulpit or from another person, but what I heard and who He is in His Word. Because of our past experiences, most of us have a biased perception of what love is. When we read the Word, we are often reading it with a wrong perception. We really need to know God's kind of love. I cannot know a friends' voice by simply getting to know them from another person and then when they call me, expect to recognize their voice. So many Christians desire and want to hear God's voice but only spend time hearing 'about Him,' not getting to know Him personally. They do not want to spend the time and effort it takes to be in His Word or spend time in His presence getting to know Him in an intimate way. Perhaps fear may even keep them from doing so, because of the way our God has been portrayed in the Church or by well meaning people.

I fell so madly in love with the Father. He is my first husband, my Daddy, my best friend, and my lover. He so loves on me. He tenderly takes my face in His hands and paints me a picture in my heart to show me all about Him. I would never have known for sure it was Him speaking to me had I not taken the time to get to know Him intimately. I certainly would have questioned the voice I heard!

I soon realized the God I had heard about in Church was not the God I met when I began to spend time with Him. I am truly sorry that many do not know His true character and even sadder that most do not even care to! Some people are even afraid to know His true character, thinking He may do something bad or reprimand them for something. Because of what we are often taught through religion, we think He is a God that will be unkind and will put some disease on us because we are not living up to the religious teachings of the Church.

How did I pray for David in that time prior to going to Utah? It wasn't on my face, travailing and moaning. I will tell you it was very simple. I took about two minutes, sometimes less and I spoke to the demons that I knew were tormenting David and stealing his life. I asked God to send people into David's days and nights that would speak 'life' into him and to use the people around him to show David what an awesome God we have and how much God loved him. It was to change my heart for David, not to change David! God did that!

When God spoke to me about marrying my husband, I had total peace, though I told God "No" at first. You see David had been an alcoholic for 20 years. I had my Daddy and I was now happy to spend my days with Him. When He called me to marry David, I thought "God, why would you ask me to marry a man who is an alcoholic?" I felt like I was betraying and cheating on my husband, (God).

God then gave me confirmation through a friend and a sister, through His Word and time with Him. I knew it was God, I just didn't want to be obedient at that time in my life. I couldn't see beyond that moment with David. God had an incredible plan far beyond what my natural eyes could see. Though I couldn't see that plan yet, I did have total peace.

God asked me to pray for three things for David, I even had to look up one of the words because I didn't know what it meant. This was another confirmation that it was God calling me to marry David. He and I had not seen one another for quite some time, though we talked occasionally. When God called me to be David's wife, He also began to put a deeper love in my heart for him, God's kind of love! After several months of the Lord waking me up at 2 a.m. and 4 a.m., He told me to go see David and I spent a few days together with him in Utah. When I first arrived and he picked me up at the airport, I was horrified by how bad he looked, puffy and bloated and drunk. He wasn't the kind of drunk who was falling down, David was a maintenance drinker. He just drank all day long, every day. Later I would discover that the times The Lord woke me to pray for David, were the times he would get up during the night and drink. David could not even make it through the night without maintaining a certain amount of alcohol in his body.

On the final day of my stay in Utah with him, I was puzzled and asked God, "Why did you bring me here?" David was acting strange that day as I was getting ready to leave. I decided I would just go for a walk before my plane left. I was getting ready when I heard a loud bang in the basement where he was getting ready. It startled me, then I heard the vilest, guttural evil sounds I have ever heard. I said "Jesus, you need to take care of this." I was on my way out the door when the Lord stopped me and said to go to the basement and check on David. I did as the Lord instructed and looked for him, calling out his name with no answer. The bathroom door was a jar, just an inch, and I peeked in to find David laying in a pool of blood with his head split open.

I think I called on Jesus first and then I called the paramedics. I didn't know all about my authority and inheritance at this time. When they arrived, they asked me where I wanted them to take David. "I'm not from here," I answered and then quickly followed it by; "Ogden Regional" I had no idea there was such a place, but of course my Daddy did. I followed the ambulance to the hospital. They began to stitch David's head and asked me lots of questions. I told them to stitch his head with my initials in it. After they finished, we were alone in the room and David went into a seizure. I yelled for the doctors and as they came in, they said "he is detoxing." How ignorant I was of alcoholism. I didn't know that a person could have seizures when they drink too much or when they are cutting back. I spoke to the mountain in David and commanded alcoholism to leave and thanked God for sparing his life. I did get angry with him for allowing the enemy to come in and nearly kill and destroy his life. The enemy stole many years of his life but I was not willing that he would die by the Enemy. Just as my Father called me to be his wife, He also said He would equip me.

David went into the detox portion of the hospital. This particular hospital had an incredible program for addicts. It was run by a man who had once belonged to a youth Christian organization, but because he fell in love with a beautiful woman of a religion not based on the word of God, he left his Christian faith and turned to another. God used that simple foundation that this man had once walked in, to run a great recovery program. The Lord moved in David's heart in a great way "and the prayers offered up in faith will heal the sick." David was sick, with Satan's lies. I spoke to the Enemy and the alcoholism. David had been saved but he didn't KNOW my Daddy like I did or have as intimate relationship with Him yet. David believed enough to go to heaven; however, he was just getting there very quickly and not very joyfully.

I left Utah and thought that perhaps that was the

only reason God spoke to me about David being my husband was to get me to visit him in order to save his life (this is intercession). I was okay with that, though I will say when I saw David before leaving, the love had grown into something I had never known. It was God's love for the man he called to be my husband. As I looked across the room at him with a baseball sized knot, and stitches in his head, black and blue and a swollen puffy face from years of alcohol, it could only be God's kind of love that filled me that day. I accepted the call to be David's wife, even though I wasn't positive he would choose to continue to follow Our Lord. If God called me, I would trust in the finished work of Jesus in David as well.

I went back to Denver and David began to drink again. He called me several months later asking if I would come and help him. I agreed, not knowing what God had planned. When you trust God, you don't have to know all the details only that He is asking you to go. In fact, had I known all the details, I probably would have said "no." When I arrived, I spent time with the Lord as David continued to drink in his basement for four days. On the fifth day, David walked upstairs and asked if I would like to witness him pouring out his last beer. I said "yes," and watched the beer go down the drain.... along with his addiction.

We sat at the table and talked that day and David said, "I suppose we should get married," I answered "Yes."

When I told my family we were getting married, they thought I was crazy. My mother said I did not serve the same God as she did, if my God told me to marry this man. I said, "He called me to marry David, not you, and He has equipped me for what lies ahead. God told me two years would be difficult." I held Him to his promise and knew that I could hold on to His Words and truth and that in two years if it wasn't what I thought it should be, I would just leave and divorce David. I will say that at the end of two years, David's and my life was incredibly blessed and David loves our Jesus, His Jesus, as I do. He may not believe yet in everything as I do, but that's ok. Well, actually, it's not okay with me. David may get to heaven before me, which is still a great benefit, I just want the man I love here to have all the same wonderful benefits of a loving God; health, joy, peace, prosperity, etc.

Had I not spent time with our Lord getting to know Him intimately, I never would have had the incredible peace I had on our wedding day. I would not have this incredible husband that God gave me, because in my own flesh, I never would have married this man the way he looked to the world. God let me see through His eyes, the man He called to be my husband here on earth.

I often tell women not to put God in a box when it comes to the man that He has for them to marry. But I follow that up with a disclaimer of sorts, that unless they are 100% sure that it is God who has called them to marry a man like my David, that they should run the other way. Those first two years had some bumpy times, but because I could hold onto the Words of my Daddy, I focused on those words during those times to get me through them. I can say it was nearly to the day of twenty four months that miraculous things happened in my husband's life. Lights began to come on for him in regards to the incredible love of Our Lord. This again is what changes lives.

I did have to move to Utah though. I fell in love with the people and the surroundings and when God called us back to Colorado, I had peace, but cried leaving friends, family, and the area we were living. When I first moved to Utah, because I had studied the region and the culture, I thought I was totally prepared! Utah was like living on a different planet. Remember, God had said, "I want you to love on them like I do." I had my neighbors asking me "What are you?" which gave me the chance to share the grace and love of our incredible God to a lost people. What a great opportunity! It was my mission field, besides being David's wife.

When we moved back to Colorado, I thought Ahhhh wonderful, "I'll be surrounded by Christians!" Oops… they just called themselves that… but many really didn't know my Jesus. I was kind of mad, seeing so many who said they were 'believers' but not believing in what Jesus has for us and did for us. Most of all, I was sad. Once again my Daddy spoke to me and said "I want you to love on them like I do, just as you did in Utah." You know what? It's harder for me to love on those that say they are believers, than those who don't. I have a higher expectation and think they should know better, and know the truth of who they are because of what Jesus did. I am still disappointed because God says, "His people perish for lack of knowledge." I don't want you or anyone else to perish for not having an understanding. I want you to be living an awesome life here, in health, joy, and peace!

Hosea 4:6 *My people are destroyed for lack of knowledge: because thou hast rejected knowledge…*

2 Timothy 2:15 *Study to shew thyself approved unto God, a workman that needeth not to be ashamed, rightly dividing the word of truth.*

John 8:32 *And ye shall know the truth, and the truth shall make you free.*

The only way you will know the Truth is by being in the Word of God, studying His Word, getting to know Him in an intimate way. It is worth it!

It's a wonderful thing to know that when God speaks to you, you know it's Him. You can trust it is Him and rely on every word He speaks. You don't even have to question; why, what, how, or when. When we start doing that, I think that we begin to negate His Word. If He thought we needed to know some of the things we are now asking, don't you think He would have told us? Rely on what He says, don't question His Word. Question those at the pulpit, and me and other teachers. The one thing we can rely on always is "His Word is Truth filled with love and grace."

John 20:31 *But these are written, that ye might believe that Jesus is the Christ, the Son of God; and that believing ye might have life through his name.*

John 6:29 *Jesus answered and said unto them, This is the work of God, that ye believe on him whom he hath sent.*

John 4:48 *Then said Jesus unto him, Except ye see signs and wonders, ye will not believe.*

Mark 9:23 *Jesus said unto him, If thou canst believe, all things are possible to him that believeth.*

2 Peter 1:2 *Grace and peace be multiplied unto you through the knowledge of God, and of Jesus our Lord,*

2 Peter 1:3 *According as his divine power hath given unto us all things that pertain unto life and godliness, through the knowledge of him that hath called us to glory and virtue:*

Prayer: "Lord, I thank you that I know you, that I hear your voice over all others and that my relationship with you is so strong that I know it is you when you speak. Help me to find the time, desire and passion to spend in your Word and to want to know you more." Amen

Chapter 4

Salvation and Healing are a Part of the Atonement, and More

"Connie, You do not even believe me to forgive you your sins, how can you believe me for your healing?"

"Yes, LORD I have committed so many horrible sins, how can you forgive all these?"

"Then I sent my Son for nothing."

As I think on this conversation with the Lord, I dwell on the fact that He called me by name! Thank you my precious Lord. He calls all of us by name.

As I think on His Words to me and as I seek His wisdom on healing and all He has for us, I realize it is not because of anything I have done, or because of the challenges I have had in my life, it is because of His Words spoken to me, because of the promises He gave us, the more, the greater He said we would be doing. It has nothing to do with what I do, but everything to do with Him and what He did. He provided everything for us through His atonement, His sacrifice on the cross on that incredible day when He died for each of us, and has now shared these truths with us in His Word.

It is my responsibility now to seek out His truths to believe and to know His promises and truth's to us. What did He do at the cross?

Hosea 4:6 *My people are destroyed for lack of knowledge.*

Many people want the greater but are not willing to put the time into receiving it. They think because God is sovereign He will just do it for them. Perhaps people think attending church once a week; they will have all they need. Many churches are not even teaching the truth of Jesus Christ, "the almost too good to be true good news," the Gospel. If you are not hearing the good news at your church, will you know the truth? You must spend time in His Word, by studying, and hearing the truth.

We can't believe right, if we have wrong knowledge.

Most of us have been taught and identify that salvation is a part of the atonement. Salvation may also be called "deliverance" or "redemption" from sin and its effects. Salvation is made possible by the life, death, and resurrection of Christ, which in the context of salvation is referred to as the "atonement."

Romans 5:11 *And not only so, but we also joy in God through our Lord Jesus Christ, by whom we have now received the atonement.*

The definition of the word atonement is: the reconciliation of God and mankind, making amends for an offense, cleansing. Atonement is a doctrine that describes how sin can be forgiven by God. It refers to the forgiving or pardoning of sin through the death of Jesus Christ by crucifixion, which made possible the reconciliation between God and creation. The word atonement was invented in the sixteenth century by William Tyndale who recognized that there wasn't a direct English translation of the biblical Hebraic concept. The word is composed of two parts "at" and "onement" it reflects the remission of sin and reconciliation of man to God.

Acts 4:12 *"Salvation is found in no one else, for there is no other name given under heaven by which we must be saved."* (These were the Lords words)

It is only through Jesus that we get to partake of this incredible gift, not Ala, Buddha, Jimbo, or any other man. There is one way to the Father and as a Christian we know it is through Jesus Christ. There is more to our Jesus' sacrificial atonement than just the remission of sin and being reconciled to Him. Tyndale's invented word left a lot out. I personally had not been taught (or I missed it somewhere) that healing, health, prosperity, freedom and forgiveness are all a part of the atonement. I am focusing more on the healing in this chapter. We'll be focusing on His atonement and how healing was brought to us and given to us through Jesus' sacrificial atonement on the cross. God says, "By His wounds I have been healed." This is not just my Spiritual healing, though it begins there. My Spirit is totally, 100% healed, prosperous, forgiven, and set free when I have a relationship with Christ. My soul and body need to come into alignment with that truth. I am able to do this through the spoken word, renewing my mind, reading, and through studying His truths. My spirit, soul and body are all 100% healed, prosperous, forgiven and set free.

1 Peter 2:24 *He Himself took our infirmities and bare our sicknesses.*

Psalm 107:20 *He sent his word, and healed them, and delivered them from their destructions.*

Isaiah 53:5-6 *But he was wounded for our transgressions, he was bruised for our iniquities: the chastisement of our peace was upon him; and with his stripes we are healed. All we like sheep have gone astray; we have turned every one to his own way; and the Lord hath laid on him the iniquity of us all.*

Religion, or perhaps it was just the church I grew up in, never mentioned the parts of salvation other than my sins were forgiven and now I get to go to heaven. Again that is an incredibly awesome gift, but He did so much more. He said we would be doing so much more.

John 14:12 *Verily, verily, I say unto you, He that believeth on me, the works that I do shall he do also; and greater works than these shall he do; because I go unto my Father.*

Just as we choose to receive and believe His salvation for us, He wants us to choose His healing, prosperity, forgiveness and freedom, which are all a part of His salvation. He's already given it all to us. He's already provided it, and He already did it. Now I must believe and receive. Yes, it's my responsibility. I do not take the place of God, but He lives inside of me.

Acts 2:4 *And they were all filled with the Holy Ghost, and began to speak with other tongues, as the Spirit gave them utterance.* (If you have not been baptized in the Holy Spirit, you need to do this. He brings the power of the Gospel)

Acts 1:8 *But ye shall receive power, after that the Holy Ghost is come upon you: and ye shall be witnesses unto me both in Jerusalem, and in all Judea, and in Samaria, and unto the uttermost part of the earth.*

Jesus gave His life so that we would have abundant life and not just in heaven, but here.

3 John 1:2 *"I wish above all else that you would prosper and be in good health."*

A loving Father only wants the best for His children! If we kept giving our child a wonderful precious gift, but they just wouldn't take it, how would that make us feel? We have minimized through religion, the sacrifice of our Jesus on the cross. He bare our sickness and diseases. What if I 'put' sickness on my child to teach them about this abundant life? How really stupid of a thought is that? I would never consider using this method of training nor would our Lord.

1 Peter 2:24 *Who his own self bare our sins in his own body on the tree, that we, being dead to sins, should live unto righteousness: by whose stripes ye were healed.*

I was cautious at first when seeking God on healing because I had seen people who were naming and claiming things that are outside of the 'laws and will of God.'

As I study His Word, I see He wants us to proclaim the things He has given us and to thank and praise Him for them. Once you get a real revelation of all that you have through His sacrifice it's nearly impossible not to live a life of praise and thanksgiving to Him. It's also nearly impossible to not believe that He has provided all the healing we are ever going to need and that we have it all now.

We cannot be claiming and receiving things outside His will. I cannot claim a new husband because I don't like the one I have. I cannot claim money into my bank account without working for it, even though He wants us all to prosper. His requirement for me is that I use my hands, the gifts I have to work with and He will bless that. He cannot bless me doing nothing. This is where you might be confused because we don't have to do anything because He did it all. Now you hear me saying He cannot bless 'nothing.' When we expect Him to do everything in our lives, it goes against what He is telling us. Yes, He provided everything for us at the cross, but then He said He was going away. He has given us the power and authority to raise the dead, heal the sick, etc. He has now transferred the power and authority over to us, He has gifted us with the Holy Spirit for wisdom and He has given us His inheritance. We are one with Him. (atonement). We don't have to use that power and authority, but what an incredible gift! It's His power and authority living inside of us, why not use it!

Some teach that miracles and healings are not for today. If this is what you believe, that's exactly what I suppose you are getting. Many of God's people are not receiving or believing in all He has said He has done for us and given us, for many reasons. We often see miracles and healings happening in third world countries. Why are we not seeing them so much here in America? Perhaps the answer is in our prosperity or perhaps in our religious teachings, or because of all the unbelief we are fed daily. We do not depend on our precious Lord. We are so accustomed to medical doctors and receiving all the 'wisdom of man' that we have not believed the wisdom of Jesus Himself and the gifts that He gave at the cross. He gave them to us. Remember, I just need to believe and receive them, not strive to achieve.

Keep going to His Word. What does He say, and do we believe it? I keep saying to myself "read it and believe it," His Word is true. There are moments when I have belief and un-belief. Just as Paul had said, "Lord help me in my un-belief." I also have prayed, "Help me Lord in my unbelief."

Mark 9:24 *Straightway the father of the child cried out, and said, I believe; help thou mine unbelief.*

I do not want to miss one thing He did for us; or have anyone else miss out on God's awesome gifts. If He provided salvation, (healing, prosperity, forgiveness, freedom) and we so desire this in our lives, why should we not desire everything He did for us at Calvary, the cross? He sacrificed His life and died for us, so that we would have life, and have it more abundantly.

John 10:10 *The thief cometh not, but that he may steal, and kill, and destroy: I came that they may have life, and may have [it] abundantly.*

Psalm 103:3 *Who forgiveth all thine iniquities; who healeth all thy diseases;*

This scripture tells me that the healing was not just a spiritual heart issue, He meant our physical body. Diseases are of the physical. So why isn't everyone healed? Is it because not all believe? Yes, says God, "If you believe." I personally am renewing my mind by immersing myself in His Word to believe. I continually feed my believer.

2 Corinthians 10:5 *"I demolish arguments and every pretension that sets itself up against the Knowledge of God and I take captive every thought to make it obedient to Christ."*

I remember repeating this scripture several times a day as the lies in my head and thoughts contradicted

God's truths. I knew I needed His Word's to overcome all those lies.

Mark 5:36 *As soon as Jesus heard the word that was spoken, he saith unto the ruler of the synagogue, be not afraid, and only believe.*

Mark 11:24 *Therefore I say unto you, What things soever ye desire, when ye pray, believe that ye receive them, and ye shall have them.* (Do you believe?)

Luke 8:50 *But when Jesus heard it, he answered him, saying, Fear not: believe only, and she shall be made whole.*

The Son of God.

Most everything you hear on TV, read in the news, see in a magazine, speaks unbelief to us.

Romans 10:17 *"For faith cometh by hearing, and hearing by the Word of God"*

I need to acknowledge what He has already provided for me. I need to hear and read the Word. Others need to hear as well. God did not tell us to pray for the sick. He says for us to pray without ceasing. He told us to "GO" heal the sick, raise the dead, and open blind eyes. To preach the Gospel to share the good news. Did you get that? He didn't tell us to ask Him to heal, He told us to do it!

Matthew 10:8 *Heal the sick, raise the dead, cleanse the lepers, cast out demons: freely ye received, freely give*

Speak His Word aloud and meditate on His Word, because He says…"say to this mountain,"

Mark 11:23 *For verily I say unto you, That whosoever shall say unto this mountain, Be thou removed, and be thou cast into the sea; and shall not doubt in his heart, but shall believe that those things which he saith shall come to pass; he shall have whatsoever he saith.*

God tells us that "sickness and disease are in the power of the tongue." Use your words to get rid of those things and not to bring them on yourselves.

Psalm 35:27 *Let them shout for joy and be glad who favor my righteous cause and them SAY continually let the Lord be magnified who has pleasure in the prosperity of his servants.*

People often believe they are not receiving God's healing and blessings in their lives, because they haven't performed well enough, prayed enough, tithed enough, they have been cursed, or simply because they missed church last week or the last year, or the many number of reasons we might have believed that were told to us. Nor do we receive healing because I spent five hours praying this morning, repented from sins, served in the community, was usher in my church, went on a mission trip, or I am the leader of worship. It has nothing to do with what we do.

We miss the healing because of our unbelief, and these things in our lives are just by products of our unbelief. I sin, because I do not believe God. God also says in Isaiah 33:24 DO NOT SAY…I am sick." Again we see power in our words, in our tongues. I am not healed because I don't have enough faith, or it's just God's will. That is a lie. God's will for me is to have health. He wrote it in His spiritual laws at the cross.

3 John 1:2 *Beloved, I pray that in all things thou mayest prosper and be in health, even as thy soul prospereth.*

He has already given me enough Faith. It is His faith, "THE faith" of God that lives inside me. I don't have to go muster some up! I hear so many Christians say, "I must not have enough faith" or "I wish I had more faith like you Connie." They do, we all do. We all have the same measure of His faith.

Hebrews 12:2 *looking unto Jesus the author and perfecter of [our] faith, who for the joy that was set before him endured the cross, despising shame, and hath sat down at the right hand of the throne of God.*

Galatians 2:20 *I have been crucified with Christ; and it is no longer I that live, but Christ living in me: and that [life] which I now live in the flesh I live in faith, [the faith] which is in the Son of God, who loved me, and gave himself up for me.*

What filter am I looking through? Due to where we have been, our teachings, the world, and many things from our past experiences, we are viewing Jesus through our own filter. We need to see Him as He says He is in His Word. Let the Word of God get in the way of your beliefs.

Producing God's results in our lives does not always require a miracle or man. It only requires my will acting on the Word, what He has done to produce the result, (atonement) or what He has already purchased. I just enforce the laws God has already put into effect.

(healing, prosperity, forgiveness, freedom.) I am the law enforcer and He is the law provider.

Producing and getting the results of His provision has been a process for me. It is taking some time to turn my ship as I heard my Pastor teach recently. Though I may not feel the ship moving, the rudder is slowly turning the ship and soon I will be face to face in the (other direction) facing my beloved Jesus and seeing, living, and believing His truths. If I believe for a healing, it will soon manifest.

Romans 13:14 *Put on the Lord Jesus Christ and make no provision for the heart set on the flesh.*

Jesus provided everything He is ever going to provide at the cross. Healing is a part of the atonement of that sacrifice. You do not have to add one thing to what He did, not works, not studying (though it is a good thing) but does not provide the healing. It helps you believe for it. Jesus is now seated at the right hand of God the Father. He is no longer healing people today. He already did it all. Remember…"It is finished!" It's all been provided for in His atonement. You have all the healing, health, prosperity and forgiveness living inside you.

You now need to believe it, renew your mind to His truths, activate your voice, and speak to the mountains in your life.

I am still renewing my mind to many truths. I have been taught so many unbelief's in my life. There are things today that my God will show me in His Word. Things I thought were truths are now just wrong teachings, traditions of the church, man-made traditions that were making the Word of God of no effect in my life. As I turn my ship and plant the seeds, I get to see His truths and begin to believe. I so want everyone else to 'get it.' What is IT? The almost too good to be true Good News of Jesus Christ. The Gospel. Health, prosperity, forgiveness, freedom, and the inheritance you have. Most of all, His incredible LOVE. We all need love. His love is more than I could ever describe in words. I will try to show you in the testimonies of my life and His Son's life given for you and me.

Ephesians 1: 17-19 *"I keep asking that You the God of My Lord Jesus Christ, my glorious Father, that you give me the spirit of wisdom and revelation so I may know YOU better. I pray also that the eyes of my heart may be enlightened in order that I may know the hope to which YOU have called me, the riches of YOUR glorious inheritance to me and YOUR incomparably great power for me - who believes...* (I changed Ephesians 1: 17-19 and made it personal, learn what God's laws are and put them into action.)

Additional scripture references

1 John 5:5 *Who is he that overcometh the world, but he that believeth that Jesus is the Son of God?*

John 11:26 *And whosoever liveth and believeth in me shall never die. Believest thou this?*

1John 5:13 *These things have I written unto you that believe on the name of the Son of God; that ye may know that ye have eternal life, and that ye may believe on the name of the Son of God.*

Romans 1:16 *For I am not ashamed of the gospel of Christ: for it is the power of God unto salvation to every one that believeth; to the Jew first, and also to the Greek.*

Romans 3:22 *Even the righteousness of God which is by faith of Jesus Christ unto all and upon all them that believe: for there is no difference.*

John 7:38 *He that believeth on me, as the scripture hath said, out of his belly shall flow rivers of living water.*

Acts 13:39 *And by him all that believe are justified from all things, from which ye could not be justified by the law of Moses.*

Acts 15:11 *But we believe that through the grace of the Lord Jesus Christ we shall be saved, even as they.*

James 2:19 *Thou believest that there is one God; thou doest well: the devils also believe, and tremble.*

1 John 3:23 *And this is his commandment, that we should believe on the name of his Son Jesus Christ, and love one another, as he gave us commandment.*

1 John 4:16 *And we have known and believed the love that God hath to us. God is love; and he that dwelleth in love dwelleth in God, and God in him.*

1 John 5:10 *He that believeth on the Son of God hath the witness in himself: he that believeth not God hath made him a liar; because he believeth not the record that God gave of his Son.*

John 6:63 *God sent His Word (Jesus) and healed them.* (Past tense)

Mark 1:8 *I indeed have baptized you with water: but he shall baptize you with the Holy Ghost.*

Acts 2:38 *Then Peter said unto them, Repent, and be baptized every one of you in the name of Jesus Christ for the remission of sins, and ye shall receive the gift of the Holy Ghost.*

Romans 15:13 *Now the God of hope fill you with all joy and peace in believing, that ye may abound in hope, through the power of the Holy Ghost.*

Psalm 33:4 *For the word of the Lord is right; and all his works are done in truth.*

1 Timothy 4:15 *Meditate upon these things; give thyself wholly to them; that thy profiting may appear to all.*

Prayer: "Thank you Lord for providing everything for me at the cross, that your work was complete. I receive everything you provided; Your health, abundant life, freedom, forgiveness and every precious gift. I love you LORD.
Amen

Chapter 5

Use the Power and Authority God Gave Us

Luke 9:1-2 *Then He called his twelve disciples together, and gave them power and authority over all devils, and to cure diseases. And He sent them to preach the Kingdom of God, and to heal the sick.*

Before you can believe that you have this same

power and authority, you need to be convinced that sickness and disease are not from God. If that is how we learn and grow, or others believe or receive their salvation through sickness and disease then why pray for healing? Why would God give us that inheritance; an inheritance of sickness and infirmities.

Does God say people receive salvation through the sickness and diseases and through their suffering? No, He says the way to salvation is in the Word, by hearing the truth. The truth is what sets you free.

John 8:32 *And ye shall know the truth, and the truth shall make you free.*

God's discipline is not sickness, disease, or infirmities. He would not have rebuked and healed and given us the power and authority over all devils to cure diseases, if He gave us these infirmities for our own good or the good of others.

Why would He ask us to go out and heal sicknesses, if they were given to teach us and others a lesson? That sounds pretty silly to me. None of us should ever go to a doctor or pray for the healing to come and be manifest in our lives if they are gifts from God. Actually we shouldn't be going to Doctors except when we are in unbelief. You do not need a Doctors report to 'prove' you have been healed. That is unbelief! Health is already yours.

I don't see anywhere in the Word that it is by sickness, diseases or trials. Before the sacrifice of Jesus Christ, God brought sickness and diseases and even killed people because of the sin that was in the world. When Jesus came, He gave us the new covenant, a covenant of grace and love and gave to us His inheritance.

God says "believe." I now have the same authority and power living on the inside of me as the 12 disciples. Yes, as Jesus himself. Jesus said we will be doing even greater things than He. Without Jesus I am nothing. But I am not 'nothing'. I am born again, spirit filled and I have Jesus living on the inside of me. Remember, it is His power and authority, not mine, I just get to appropriate it!

Luke 17:21 *The Kingdom of God is within me. Neither shall they say, Lo, here! or, There! for lo, the kingdom of God is within you.*

Acts 1:8 *"But you will receive power when the Holy Spirit comes on you, and you will be my witness..."*

John 14:12-14 *Verily, verily, I say unto you, he that believeth on me, the works that I do shall he do also; and greater [works] than these shall he do; because I go unto the Father. And whatsoever ye shall ask in my name, that will I do, that the Father may be glorified in the Son. If ye shall ask anything in my name, that will I do.*

Are we doing greater things? Not too many! Not yet anyway. That may sound arrogant, but my God says we will. We just had not believed or known this before, so I am expecting 'great' things and have already seen many, but I want to see many more. (We will never have the gifts of healing and the working miracles in operation unless we stand in the divine power that God gives us, unless we stand believing God and "having done all" (Eph 6:13), we still stand believing. Smith Wigglesworth)

There is nothing that can interfere with our coming into perfect blessing except unbelief. Unbelief is a terrible obstacle, but oh how much of our human reasoning we have to get rid of. How many of us believe the WORD? It is easy for us to quote it, but it is more important to 'have' it than to quote it. The life of the Son is in us and God wants us to believe. Oh, what privileges are ours when we are Born of God! We don't have to take these privileges, they will not keep us out of heaven if we are not walking in all He has for us. But there are multitudes who need this Greater, or even the things Jesus did. They need to experience healing in their lives, emotionally, spiritually, physically. We need to be doing even what He did and then go on to the greater! If we do not tell people, how will they know? If one of you reading this is saved from an eternity in hell, healed or set free in any way because of our obedience and belief, how glorious! What joy our Father receives, what glory is His! We want all eyes on Him not on us or anyone else. We are doing the greater to bring glory to Him. It is His desire to work in and through us.

Phil. 2:13 …'*for His good pleasure'*.

Because I had believed the lies and deception of the Enemy, I was waiting and praying for God to do the things He told me to do. He said He was going away and that he was leaving with us the Holy Spirit and when His power came upon us we would be doing great things. We now have the power and authority to raise the dead, heal the sick, cast out demons - and even greater things. What GREATER things could we be doing? We see Peter who had some of this 'greater' when even as his shadow passed over people they were healed. (Acts 5:12-16 Acts 19:11-12 Acts 8:13) Oh what a glorious day when you realize we have been given this 'greater' power. You simply have not taken it, or believed you even have it to take. God has given us the gift of His Son, and all that comes with that, His death, burial and resurrection power - to heal the sick, raise the dead, cast our demons, drink deadly poison without it harming us..... It is not me, but Christ in me that is the POWER and the AUTHORITY! The Name of Jesus has power.

As I study these incredible truths, and renew my mind to all I have as a believer, I have not yet arrived, meaning I am not always successful in seeing healings in my life or others manifest, but I'm on my way and I expect them to be happening more and I expect the greater things He said we would be doing to start happening as well. (Phil. 3:12-13). What could we be doing that would be greater? Our shadows healing the sick, transporting ourselves to another city? Oh, now Connie you have gone off the deep end. This sounds pretty crazy to most of you. We should be doing the greater things.

I have heard people say and have even said things myself in the past such as, "well you know God says we will have afflictions and hard times, to teach us. We live in this fallen world. It is part of being a Christian." Or, "Don't you think God gave us doctors to heal us now?" My God is saying to me, if I am sick, call on the elders to pray and anoint me, or simply do it myself. James 5:14-15. I have that same power over any sickness that may try to come against me. I am going from healing to living in health. He didn't say go see a doctor and have them cut off body parts to save you from sickness. This is exactly what I did. I needed a doctor at the time, I was walking in unbelief. His word doesn't say to me that I will need to take pharmaceuticals to keep me alive. Praise God there are drugs available for you when your unbelief and thinking is of the world and not on the things of God. It is as I have said before. It is MY lack of knowledge, wrong teaching, and leaning on my five senses that brings in this kind of thinking. We still have an Enemy that would use lies and deception to lead us to believe these things - the things of the world and not of God. God did say we would face trials and persecutions because of our faith, not sickness and disease unto death. I have studied the scriptures on trials and persecutions. I see the believer will face these. They are because of our belief in Christ, they are governmental trials, persecutions, of imprisonment, perhaps even beatings for our belief in Christ, but I could not see that they were sickness and diseases. His wish, His desire is for all HIS people (believers) to be in good health. However, He says, IF any of you are sick, call on the elders, speak to your mountain.

James 5:14-15 *Is any sick among you? let him call for the elders of the church; and let them pray over him, anointing him with oil in the name of the Lord: And the prayer of faith shall save the sick, and the Lord shall raise him up; and if he have committed sins, they shall be forgiven him.*

The word saved is translated Sozo, which means healed, prosperous, forgiven and set free.

Romans 10:17 *So then faith cometh by hearing, and hearing by the word of God.*

I have yet to see in His Word since Jesus came that faith comes through sickness, disease and testing by God.

Phil. 3:12 *Not that I have already obtained all this, or have already been made perfect, but I press on to take hold of that for which Christ Jesus took hold of me.*

I want you to be on your way as well. Jesus loves us. He would no more send us sickness and disease to teach us than we would on our own child or loved one. Though I had someone say that they would break their child's arm, or put cancer on him if it would teach him a lesson. They followed that by saying " You never know how God will use that." As Andrew Wommack has said,

"How dumb can you be and still breathe." I say you should be arrested for child abuse! My God says it is by His Word that we learn and grow. We do not grow by a broken arm or cancer.

John 8:32 *and ye shall know the truth, and the truth shall make you free.*

I believe we can learn things during such a time, but only because this is when people usually seek the Lord in their lives, and not before. It is not God's way to help you grow. He has a BETTER way! When we represent God in such a way to the world, as a loving God and if we were actually doing the things God tells us and we walked in the Power and authority, we would see many more in the world turning to a loving, gracious, patient God. People would not be running from an angry, judgmental God who is ready to put sickness on His people to teach them a lesson. Another ridiculous 'religious teaching.'

God has given us the power to heal the sick (even ourselves). I believe sickness and disease try to come upon us and will continue to, but we do not have to take it on. "Believe that ye receive and ye shall have whatever you ask."

Mark 11:24 *Therefore I say unto you, What things soever ye desire, when ye pray, believe that ye receive them, and ye shall have them.*

I believe that in this scripture it is also talking about such things as sickness and diseases. If you ask for sickness and disease, you will probably get it. There is an example of a young man who asked for cancer to be able to use it to minister to others in need. He became sick and died of cancer. We are told that people 'gave their lives to Christ at his funeral.' They said it is proof that God uses these things to bring glory to Him. What Glory is that? A young man in his youth dies. The people who were saved were not saved because of his death, but because someone most likely spoke something at the funeral, perhaps it was the Gospel, that brought them to an understanding to receive salvation, or maybe out of fear of going to hell when they die.

I believe for things in some areas more than others. Since I have entertained the flesh in a certain area for a long time, it is harder for my mind to be renewed in these areas. Sometimes it takes time to renew our thinking, our minds, to be like Christ. But it also takes effort. If I am not making the effort, my mind will be stayed on the things of this world, it will be focused on my five senses.

There are those who like sickness and have lived with it for so long, it is common and even comfortable. I have seen that I have nested in this area in my own life. Others like the attention sickness brings to them. God wants a different attention. He wants the attention from the power and authority He gives us to raise the dead and heal the sick. It is He whom the Glory should be given. When we as Christians are raising the dead, healing the sick, staying well, living in the blessings, this brings much more glory to our Lord. Glory does not happen when we look and act like the rest of the world. I may sound harsh here. I may sound insensitive to those of you who have lost loved ones who are experiencing sickness. (please know I am talking to myself). As I said, I haven't yet arrived...but again, I am on my way. I do not obviously have all the answers, only God does. I know they are in His Word and are found in Him.

2 Tim. 3:16-17 *Every scripture inspired of God [is] also profitable for teaching, for reproof, for correction, for instruction which is in righteousness. That the man of God may be complete, furnished completely unto every good work.*

Col 2:2-3 *that their hearts may be comforted, they being knit together in love, and unto all riches of the full assurance of understanding, that they may know the mystery of God, [even] Christ, in whom are all the treasures of wisdom and knowledge hidden.*

Why do I spend so much time in His Word and with Him? To get to know His truths and Him, because He is my best friend, my Daddy and I want to know everything about Him. KNOW his truths. KNOW, KNOW, KNOW -- BELIEVE, BELIEVE, BELIEVE. I want my total inheritance, but if I don't know what it is that I have inherited as a believer, I cannot collect it. I encourage you all to search the scriptures, get to know our Jesus, and share what He shows you, with me and others.

Col 3:15-17 *And let the peace of Christ rule in your hearts, to the which also ye were called in one body; and be ye thankful. Let the word of Christ dwell in you richly; in all wisdom teaching and admonishing one another with psalms [and] hymns [and] spiritual songs, singing with grace in your hearts unto God. And whatsoever ye do, in word or in deed, [do] all in the name of the Lord Jesus, giving thanks to God the Father through him.*

There are times when I read God's Word but I don't always know it because of many factors. These factors include unbelief, wrong teaching, lack of understanding and knowledge, lies and deception of the

Enemy, or relying on my five senses. I want to rely on my sixth sense, which is the power and authority of the Holy Spirit. I want to release that power and authority, not just for my own health and prosperity and wholeness, but for the body of Christ, the Church, for those who are in need of salvation, and healing and financial wholeness. I do not want to teach wrong, powerless faith and wrong belief.

The gifts of healing and raising the dead are not just for a chosen few or even a chosen 'many.' They are for ALL who believe.

John 14:12-14 *Verily, verily, I say unto you, He that believeth on me, the works that I do shall he do also; and greater works than these shall he do; because I go unto my Father. And whatsoever ye shall ask in my name, that will I do, that the Father may be glorified in the Son. If ye shall ask any thing in my name, I will do it.*

Many Christians' hearts are right; it's our heads that are wrong. (Again, speaking to myself.)

The Bible is our owner's manual, it is my certificate of inheritance. I know most of us, like myself, don't like to read the manuals given to us with our cars and products that we purchase. But this is life and death. Perhaps not even my own right now, but someone else's (there is life and death in the power of the tongue.)

Proverbs 18:21 *Death and life are in the power of the tongue: and they that love it shall eat the fruit thereof.*

It is through His Word that I am set free -- free from sickness and all curses. I personally want to know when I am speaking according to His Word and life, or when I am speaking my own beliefs, misunderstandings and death, so that I can change! The only place I know to find these truths is in the Word of God.

The Gospel is the Power of God -- it's the 'Good News,' not, the okay news or the powerless news, or a very good story, but the Good News.

Romans 1:16 *For I am; not ashamed of the gospel of Christ: for it is the power of God unto Salvation to every one that believeth;*

Salvation is not just going to heaven when you leave this body and world. Heaven is here and now. God wants you to have 'Heaven on Earth' because it is for today. Our earth is our bodies and Christ living in us is our Heaven in our earth. Did you get that? Our earth is our bodies and Christ living in us is our Heaven in our earth.

The Word of God needs to be planted in your heart, then it comes alive and releases Power. You need to make God's Word first and foremost in your life. The Word produces fruit. We release our authority in words.

Mark 11:23 *For verily I say unto you, That whosoever shall say unto this mountain, Be thou removed, and be thou cast into the sea; and shall not doubt in his heart, but shall believe that those things which he saith shall come to pass; he shall have whatsoever he saith.*

I want the Word to dominate my life so I am careful of what I watch, what I speak, what I hear and what I look at. The more grounded I am in Christ and His truths, the less I am effected by all the lies and negative words spoken in the world and to me.

Understanding takes effort. We are in a battle. God wants us to actively fight against the lies of the Enemy and the stealing of our time, to the mindless or worldly things that bring and feed unbelief in our lives instead of belief. Most people's faith is not in the Word of God but on the things of this world -- our emotions and on our five senses.

(Is 35:4-5 Matthew 11:4-15, Matthew 8:5-13, Isaiah 53:4-6) Resist the devil and he will flee from you. Satan comes to steal, kill and destroy, Jesus came to bring life and life more abundantly.

John 10:10. Anything of death that is of no good is of Satan. Sickness, diseases, poverty…. and anything that is good is of God. (1Tim 4:4-8, 3 John 11) Health, prosperity, wellness, joy, peace…..

If we are not born again and we are looking at the things of the 'world', then we may not see things as God has intended for us to see them.

We are blinded by the enemy until we are born again. (Give our lives to Christ, making Him our Lord and Savior.) And even then, the Enemy can blind us to the truth because we do not know what the truth is, and what God's Word says.

Hosea 4:6a *My people are destroyed for lack of knowledge:*

We are the ones who give Satan the power over us to blind us from the truth because we do not know God's truth. Satan can only do what we allow him, through his lies and deception. The only way I can perceive his lies and deception is by knowing the truth. And we know the truth through studying God's Word.

Romans 10:17 *So then faith cometh by hearing, and hearing by the word of God.*

If we are not believing God has already healed us, or we believe that God in His sovereignty chooses today who gets healed and who doesn't (it's the 'luck of the draw' or 'you know it's just because today he chose to heal Suzy and not Fred.) Or maybe Fred sinned this morning, so he was unworthy of God's healing! These are lies, lies, and more lies from the Enemy. God has already healed everyone He is ever going to heal at the cross 2000 years ago -- He has forgiven all of our sins. We now need to take the power and authority He's given us and command what is 'legally' ours. God has put certain laws into action, just as He did gravity. It is not His fault if I do not turn on, or tap into the power supply. But first I must know and understand what is mine -- what He has already given me -- what He has already done.

What is it that HE has already done?

There are certain laws that God has put into effect, such as the law of gravity. It is up to us to 'obey' those laws. If I jump off a high bridge thinking the laws of gravity do not pertain to me, I will either die or be very seriously hurt .

I am not referring to the Old Testament Laws. Our God sent His Son Jesus to Pay the price for us, and we are no longer living under 'the Law' but under Grace. This Grace is a law that we get to partake of now.

Listed here are a few of the other wonderful advantages we get to have as a believer. We first need to choose to believe and receive them.

1. FORGIVENESS OF SINS (Salvation)

John 3:16-18 *For God so loved the world, that he gave his only begotten Son, that whosoever believeth in him should not perish, but have everlasting life. For God sent not his Son into the world to condemn the world; but that the world through him might be saved. He that believeth on him is not condemned: but he that believeth not is condemned already, because he hath not believed in the name of the only begotten Son of God.*

Acts 2:21 *And it shall come to pass, that whosoever shall call on the name of the Lord shall be saved.*

The word saved as it is used here is again that translation of Sozo, which means, healed, prosperous, forgiven and set free. We are often guilty of thinking saved is about us just going to heaven when we leave this world. Being saved is so much more.

Joel 2:32 *And it shall come to pass, that whosoever shall call on the name of the Lord shall be delivered: for in mount Zion and in Jerusalem shall be deliverance, as the Lord hath said, and in the remnant whom the Lord shall call.*

Joshua 24:15 *And if it seem evil unto you to serve the Lord, choose you this day whom ye will serve; whether the gods which your fathers served that were on the other side of the flood, or the gods of the Amorites, in whose land ye dwell: but as for me and my house, we will serve the Lord.* Choose!

Romans 10:9-13, *That if thou shalt confess with thy mouth the Lord Jesus, and shalt believe in thine heart that God hath raised him from the dead, thou shalt be saved. For with the heart man believeth unto righteousness; and with the mouth confession is made unto salvation. For the scripture saith, Whosoever believeth on him shall not be ashamed. For there is no difference between the Jew and the Greek: for the same*

Lord over all is rich unto all that call upon him. For whosoever shall call upon the name of the Lord shall be saved.

Col 2:13-14 *And you, being dead in your sins and the uncircumcision of your flesh, hath he quickened together with him, having forgiven you all trespasses; Blotting out the handwriting of ordinances that was against us, which was contrary to us, and took it out of the way, nailing it to his cross;*

I am the only one who releases the power of salvation, by choosing salvation, (healing, forgiveness, freedom and prosperity.) But, I must 'choose' it. What an incredible gift.

I remember being told as a young girl in church that God chooses who is saved. I thought at the time, "why bother then to read or share the Word if God has already determined all that. How stupid is that?

Deut. 30:19 *I have set before you life and death, blessings and cursings therefore choose life, that both thou and thy seed may live.*

Prayer: "I confess with my mouth, Jesus is Lord and believe in my heart that Jesus was raised from the dead.

Thank you for your Son and for forgiving me of all my sins, I confess that I am a sinner and need a savior." Amen.

2. BAPTISM OF THE HOLY SPIRIT

The Baptism of the Holy Spirit is what releases the power, authority, and understanding given to us. The Holy spirit is my comforter and shows me the truth. It is through the Holy Spirit that we have revelation knowledge.

John 14:16-17 *And I will pray the Father, and he shall give you another Comforter, that he may abide with you for ever; Even the Spirit of truth; whom the world cannot receive, because it seeth him not, neither knoweth him: but ye know him; for he dwelleth with you, and shall be in you.*

John 14:26 *But the Comforter, which is the Holy Ghost, whom the Father will send in my name, he shall teach you all things, and bring all things to your remembrance, whatsoever I have said unto you.*

John 15:26 *But when the Comforter is come, whom I will send unto you from the Father, even the Spirit of truth, which proceedeth from the Father, he shall testify of me:*

Acts 2:4 *And they were all filled with the Holy Ghost, and began to speak with other tongues, as the Spirit gave them utterance.*

1 Cor. 14:39-40 *Wherefore, brethren, covet to prophesy, and forbid not to speak with tongues. Let all things be done decently and in order.*

Remember, we have to take it to release it...I am the only one who releases the power of the Holy Spirit by choosing to receive it. It is God's power, not mine, but He has given it to me and it is His power inside of me. Do not be afraid -- fear is not of God. Speaking in tongues may seem strange to you and may be something new. Ask God and He will not give you something you don't want; you will not receive something you don't believe in. Speaking in tongues is the power that sometimes gets me to that next level of receiving my healing. At times when I am not sure how to pray for something, I will pray in tongues. This is between me and my Father in heaven. Tongues are also used for the unbelievers. This is when you need to have an interpretation. If tongues are spoken in the body of Christ or in the church, an interpretation needs to come for the unbelievers.

1 Corinthians 14:22-25 *Wherefore tongues are for a sign, not to them that believe, but to them that believe not: but prophesying serveth not for them that believe not, but for them which believe. If therefore the whole church be come together into one place, and all speak with tongues, and there come in those that are unlearned, or unbelievers, will they not say that ye are mad? But if all prophesy, and there come in one that believeth not, or one unlearned, he is convinced of all, he is judged of all: And thus are the secrets of his heart made manifest; and so falling down on his face he will worship God, and report that God is in you of a truth.*

Ask God for the Baptism of the Holy Spirit, it is not the same as the Baptism by water, though it can happen at the same time. After you have asked, then begin by practicing speaking in tongues. It almost seemed fake to me when I began to do this. I was in the shower after I had asked for prayer for the Baptism of the Holy Spirit and I began to sing in tongues. It was strange and yet very beautiful to me. I continued to practice until it became natural to me, and then just as one language became familiar to me it seemed I would speak in another one!

Acts 18:16,17 *Because the Holy Spirit had not yet come upon any of them they had simply been baptized into the*

Name of the LORD Jesus. Then Peter and John placed their hands on them, and they received the Holy Spirit.

Mark 16:17 *And these signs shall follow them that believe; In my name shall they cast out devils; they shall speak with new tongues;*

Acts 8:14-17 *Now when the apostles which were at Jerusalem heard that Samaria had received the word of God, they sent unto them Peter and John: Who, when they were come down, prayed for them, that they might receive the Holy Ghost: (For as yet he was fallen upon none of them: only they were baptized in the name of the Lord Jesus.) Then laid they their hands on them, and they received the Holy Ghost.*

3.   POWER AND AUTHORITY IS FOR EVERY BELIEVER

When I first became aware that God's power and authority were mine to have and I began to operate in this power and authority, I had people around me who thought I was blaspheming God and going to hell for the way I spoke. Not one of those who are making these accusations had been spending time in relationship with our Lord, reading or studying the Word or spending much time with Him. So I didn't take their criticism to heart. I do take things to God when I am questioned on anything that I believe to be His truths, and you need to do the same. I never take a pastor's, teacher's, or leader's words as gospel. Check everything you see, read and hear with the Word of God.

Col. 2:9-10 *For in him dwelleth all the fullness of the Godhead bodily. And ye are complete in him, which is the head of all principality and power:*

Luke 9:1-2 *Then he called his twelve disciples together, and gave them power and authority over all devils, and to cure diseases. And he sent them to preach the kingdom of God, and to heal the sick.*

Matthew 10:1 *And when he had called unto him his twelve disciples, he gave them power against unclean spirits, to cast them out, and to heal all manner of sickness and all manner of disease.*

Begin to exercise that power and authority God has given us through the sacrifice of His Son Christ Jesus. Practice healing the sick, raising the dead, and opening blind eyes. If you don't see the manifestation right away don't you or the person you have just prayed for get into unbelief and abort the miracle. Read Daniel chapter 9.

Mark 11:23 *For verily I say unto you, That whosoever shall say unto this mountain, Be thou removed, and be thou cast into the sea; and shall not doubt in his heart, but shall believe that those things which he saith shall come to pass; he shall have whatsoever he saith.*

Release your Power and Authority in the words you speak. The spoken Word can release that power. I often speak scriptures aloud. It just seems that the Word should be spoken out loud. He didn't say the, "thought of word" or "the word I had on my mind." He said it was the Spoken word, to speak to the mountain, not think to the mountain. I am not saying that thinking something has no power, it just seems to me there is power in those spoken out loud words I use from Him. Maybe the Enemy can't hear my thoughts? Maybe I just think he can't, so when I take authority over the darkness, and the lies of the Enemy, I want to say it out loud so he can hear!

4. HEALING IS FOR EVERYONE

1 Peter 2:24 *Who his own self bare our sins in his own body on the tree, that we, being dead to sins, should live unto righteousness: by whose stripes ye were healed.*

Matthew 8:17 *That it might be fulfilled which was spoken by Esaias the prophet, saying, Himself took our infirmities, and bare our sicknesses.*

We need to release the healing power and authority Jesus Provided for us on the cross. Resist sickness; resist the devil. We need to take an active stance here by resisting.

James 4:7 *Submit yourselves therefore to God. Resist the devil, and he will flee from you.*

God tells us to submit to His truths and resist (actively fight against) the devil. We cannot be passive observers in the battle that comes against us, the thoughts and symptoms that he will 'try' to bring on you. I have shared with you that I often speak to the things that are trying to come against me right away.

It is easier to fight immediately and not wait until I am bloodied or until the thing has gotten a tight grip on me. My battle is easier when I fight against it at the first sign a pain or symptom or thought occurs.

I have found though that others want me to 'be human' as they have said. This means they want me to let the sickness come instead of thanking and praising

God right away for the healing. I would much rather my friends and family thank God for my healing than try to comfort my 'fevered brow' or give me sympathy and pity. To me that is saying my Jesus didn't do much at the cross for me, and now my friends and family have to just comfort me in my affliction. It slaps my Jesus in the face with saying what He did wasn't enough. Satan must love this!

Do not indulge sickness (entertain it, or think on it). This has been harder for me in some areas of my life than other areas. "Lord, renew my mind." It's sometimes hard not to focus on an ache or pain, but He wants us to speak to the mountain and not just entertain the mountain. Take our authority and release our healing and power. Again this is His power and His authority living inside of us as believers in Jesus Christ. He gives it to us to use.

5. FINANCIAL PROSPERITY

Many believers think our prosperity is only in the Spiritual. As we read some of the following Scriptures we see this prosperity is also financial, in health and every imaginable way. God has given us everything in the spirit, and then it needs to come out in the physical: health, prosperity, freedom, and forgiveness.

2 Corinthians 8:9 *For ye know the grace of our Lord Jesus Christ, that, though he was rich, yet for your sakes he became poor, that ye through his poverty might be rich.*

2 Corinthians 9:11 *Being enriched in every thing to all bountifulness, which causeth through us thanksgiving to God.*

Proverbs 10:4 *He becometh poor that dealeth with a slack hand: but the hand of the diligent maketh rich.*

Greed will short circuit the blessings that God has for us. He cannot bless greed.

We need to make it come to pass. Believe and receive the riches of His glorious inheritance to us. Salvation, prosperity, healing, forgiveness and freedom. Yes, He tells us in Proverbs 10:4 that we need to put our hands to diligence to become rich in finances.

6. EMOTIONAL STABILITY

One of the fruits of the Spirit is peace, which to me translates into emotional stability, and includes joy, peace, patience, kindness, and self control. None of those fruits speak of instability in our emotions. People who are emotionally unstable have a knowledge issue. They do not have a correct understanding of Jesus, and whom they are in Him, and what they have in Him. If they truly understood how much they are loved, it would be almost impossible to be emotionally depressed or unstable. He says we have, 'the mind of Christ,' if you knew that, your thoughts would begin to line up with what He says we have.

When I read this in the scriptures, I knew that I was not thinking like Christ at that time. How was I to renew my mind and to begin to have His thoughts? When I read the word and studied all the scriptures I could find on having His thoughts and mind, my thoughts began to change. If you have a problem in some area of your life, start studying those scriptures that pertain to that problem. If it's health, read every scripture about what God says on healing and health, if it's emotional read everything He says about your thoughts, and mind, about peace and joy. The word works. We can have what we say or we can say what we have. Start speaking what you have because of what He did for you.

Galatians 5:22 *But the fruit of the Spirit is love, joy, peace, longsuffering, gentleness, goodness, faith.*

If we don't have all the fruits of the spirit, it's because we are not taking them. When the Enemy brings lies of depression, remind him of who you are, and what you have in Christ: peace, joy, and love. Use your authority to release these gifts of the spirit. Seek God's presence not the fruits, and then love, joy, peace, patience, health, prosperity and all the fruits of the spirit will come. What I mean is for you to seek to be in God's presence and to know Him intimately, not to seek to be happy and joyful and have the peace. When you know Him and what you have in Him, those things will begin to have you! Amen

Proverbs 17:22 *A merry heart doeth good like a medicine: but a broken spirit drieth the bones*

Psalms 16:11 *Thou wilt shew me the path of life: in thy presence is fulness of joy; at thy right hand there are pleasures for evermore.* (not just for the hereafter!)

Isaiah 28:12 *To whom he said, This is the rest wherewith ye may cause the weary to rest; and this is the refreshing: yet they would not hear.*

Choose to do this -- clothe yourself with His truth's of who you are by seeking God.

Psalms 16:11 *You have made known to me the path of life; you will fill me with joy in your presence, with eternal pleasures at your right hand.* (this is for here and now, not just in heaven!)

7. RIGHTEOUSNESS OR JUSTIFICATION & SANCTIFICATION

Righteousness is a free gift -- it is the judicial act of God by which He pardons all the sins of those who believe in Jesus Christ. He accounts for, accepts, and treats them as righteous in the eye of the law, i.e., as conformed to all its demands. In addition to the pardon of sin, justification declares that all the claims of the law are satisfied in respect of the justified, which is all of us who believe.

The Hebrew word for righteousness is tseh'-dek, tzedek, Gesenius's righteous, integrity, equity, justice, straightness.

Romans 6:2-7 *God forbid. How shall we, that are dead to sin, live any longer therein? Know ye not, that so many of us as were baptized into Jesus Christ were baptized into his death? Therefore we are buried with him by baptism into death: that like as Christ was raised up from the dead by the glory of the Father, even so we also should walk in newness of life. For if we have been planted together in the likeness of his death, we shall be also in the likeness of his resurrection: Knowing this, that our old man is crucified with him, that the body of sin might be destroyed, that henceforth we should not serve sin. For he that is dead is freed from sin.*

We will be doing the good works when we see that we are justified, righteous and holy. We do not do good works to become justified, righteous and holy.

Romans 6:14 *For sin shall not have dominion over you: for ye are not under the law, but under grace.*

Romans 7:6 *But now we are delivered from the law, that being dead wherein we were held; that we should serve in newness of spirit, and not in the oldness of the letter.*

Sanctification is brought about by the power of the truth -- it is the work of the Holy Spirit bringing the whole nature more and more under the influences of God's grace. In other words, sanctification is the carrying on to perfection, the work begun in regeneration; and it extends to the whole man. It doesn't stop at our spirit man. To sanctify is literally "to set apart for special use or purpose," figuratively "to make holy or sacred,"

Romans 6:13 *Neither yield ye your members as instruments of unrighteousness unto sin: but yield yourselves unto God, as those that are alive from the dead, and your members as instruments of righteousness unto God.*

1 Corinthians 6:19 *What? know ye not that your body is the temple of the Holy Ghost which is in you, which ye have of God, and ye are not your own?*

The Holy Spirit in us is the plan of redemption to carry on this work. What a wonderful gift He has left with us. He said He was leaving with us something better than He. But our finite minds often have a difficult time comprehending something greater than Jesus.

1 Corinthians 6:11 *And such were some of you: but ye are washed, but ye are sanctified, but ye are justified in the name of the Lord Jesus, and by the Spirit of our God.*

Galatians 2:20 *I am crucified with Christ: nevertheless I live; yet not I, but Christ liveth in me: and the life which I now live in the flesh I live by the faith of the Son of God, who loved me, and gave himself for me.*

Romans 5:17,18 *For if by one man's offence death reigned by one; much more they which receive abundance of grace and of the gift of righteousness shall reign in life by one, Jesus Christ.) Therefore as by the offence of one judgment came upon all men to condemnation; even so by the righteousness of one the free gift came upon all men unto justification of life.*

We cannot try to earn Righteousness or sanctification ourselves. We could never do enough, be good enough, sacrifice enough. It is another of His free gifts to us.

Romans 10: 9,10 *If thou shalt confess with thy mouth the Lord Jesus, and shalt believe in thine heart that God hath raised him from the dead, thou shalt be saved. For with the heart man believeth unto righteousness; and with the mouth confession is made unto salvation.*

Romans 10:13 *For whosoever shall call upon the name of the Lord shall be saved.*

God wants us all to:
Be saved
Be prosperous
Be healed, and walk in health
Receive the Power of the Holy Spirit (with evidence of speaking in tongues)
Walk in His power and authority

Be emotionally stable. (joyful, peaceful, loving)
Walk in Righteousness and Sanctification

He desires fellowship with us. It is hard to fellowship with someone when you are trying to 'prove' yourself to them. I need to press my rights through an intimate relationship with our Lord.

2 Corinthians 1:20 *All the promises are "Yes" and "Amen" to those who believe.*

Prayer:
"I keep asking that You the God of my LORD Jesus Christ, our glorious Father, that You give me the Spirit of wisdom and revelation (and understanding) that I may know You better.

I pray also that the eyes of my heart may be enlightened in order that I may know the hope to which You have called me, the riches of Your glorious inheritance to me and Your incomparably great power for me, who believes."

Ephesians 1:17-19a "Lord, help me to see what YOU have already done." Amen

Additional Scripture References.

Romans 10:13 *For whosoever shall call upon the name of the Lord shall be saved.*

Luke 9:1-2 *Then He called his twelve disciples together, and gave them power and authority over all devils, and to cure diseases. And He sent them to preach the Kingdom of God, and to heal the sick.*

1 John 4:4 *Ye are of God, little children, and have overcome them: because greater is he that is in you, than he that is in the world.*

Matthew 10:1 *And when He had called unto him his twelve disciples, he gave them power against unclean spirits, to cast them out, and to heal all manner of sickness and all manner of disease.*

Luke 10:9 *And heal the sick that are therein, and say unto them, The kingdom of God is come nigh unto you.*

Luke 10:19 *Behold I give unto you power to tread on serpents and scorpions, and over all the power of the enemy: and nothing shall by any means hurt you.*

2 Peter 1:3 *According as his divine power hath given unto us all things that pertain unto life and godliness, through the knowledge of him that hath called us to glory and virtue:*

Matthew 10:7-8 *Heal the sick, cleanse the lepers, raise the dead, cast out devils: freely ye have received, freely give.*

James 5:14-15 *Is any sick among you? Let him call for the elders of the church; and let them pray over him, anointing him with oil in the Name of the Lord: And the prayer of faith shall save the sick, and the Lord shall raise him up; and if he have committed sins, they shall be forgiven him.*

2 Peter 1:2-3 *Grace and peace be multiplied unto you through the knowledge of God, and of Jesus our Lord, According as his divine power hath given unto us all things that pertain unto life and godliness, through the knowledge of him that hath called us to glory and virtue. Whereby are given unto us exceeding great and precious promises: that by these ye might be partakers of the divine nature, having escaped the corruption that is in the world through lust.*

John 14:12-14 *Verily, verily, I say unto you, He that believeth on me, the works that I do shall he do also; and greater works than these shall he do; because I go unto my Father. And whatsoever ye shall ask in my name, that will I do, that the Father may be glorified in the Son. If ye shall ask anything in my name, I will do it.*

John 15:16 *Ye have not chosen me, but I have chosen you, and ordained you, that ye should go and bring forth fruit, and that your fruit should remain: that whatsoever ye shall ask of the Father in my name, he may give it you.*

Mark 16:17 *And these signs will accompany those who believe; In my name you will drive out demons; they will speak in new tongues; they will pick up snakes with their hands and when they drink deadly poison it will not hurt them at all. They will place their hands on sick people and they will get well.*

3 John 1:4 *I have no greater joy than to hear that my children walk in truth.*

John 16:13-14 *Howbeit when he, the Spirit of truth, is come, he will guide you into all truth: for he shall not speak of himself; but whatsoever he shall hear, that shall he speak: and he will shew you things to come. He shall glorify me: for he shall receive of mine, and shall shew it unto you.*

John 7:3-7 *Jesus answered and said unto him, Verily, verily, I say unto thee, Except a man be born again, he cannot see the kingdom of God. Nicodemus saith unto him, How can a man be born when he is old? Can he enter the second time into his mother's womb, and be born? Jesus answered, Verily, verily, I say unto thee, Except a man be born of water and of the Spirit, he cannot enter into the kingdom of God. That which is born of the flesh is flesh; and that which is born of the Spirit is spirit. Marvel not that I said unto thee, Ye must be born again.*

Luke 10:19 *Behold, I give unto you power to tread on serpents and scorpions, and over all the power of the enemy: and nothing shall by any means hurt you.*

2 Peter 1:33 *According as his divine power hath given unto us all things that pertain unto life and godliness, through the knowledge of him that hath called us to glory and virtue:*

Acts 1:8 *But ye shall receive power, after that the Holy Ghost is come upon you: and ye shall be witnesses unto me both in Jerusalem, and in all Judaea, and in Samaria, and unto the uttermost part of the earth.*

John 14:12-14 *Verily, verily, I say unto you, He that believeth on me, the works that I do shall he do also; and greater works than these shall he do; because I go unto my Father. And whatsoever ye shall ask in my name, that will I do, that the Father may be glorified in the Son. If ye shall ask any thing in my name, I will do it.*

Col. 3:12-13 *Put on therefore, as the elect of God, holy and beloved, bowels of mercies, kindness, humbleness of mind, meekness, longsuffering; Forbearing one another, and forgiving one another, if any man have a quarrel against any: even as Christ forgave you, so also do ye.*

Colossians 3:10 *And have put on the new man, which is renewed in knowledge after the image of him that created him:*

2 Thessalonians 2:13 *But we are bound to give thanks always to God for you, brethren beloved of the Lord, because God hath from the beginning chosen you to salvation through sanctification of the Spirit and belief of the truth:*

Ephesians 1:17-19 *That the God of our Lord Jesus Christ, the Father of glory, may give unto you the spirit of wisdom and revelation in the knowledge of him: The eyes of your understanding being enlightened; that ye may know what is the hope of his calling, and what the riches of the glory of his inheritance in the saints, And what is the exceeding greatness of his power to us-ward who believe, according to the working of his mighty power*

Chapter 6
The Words of My Mouth

God -"Connie, you do not even believe me to forgive you your sins, how can you believe me for your healing?"

Me- "But God, I have committed so many sins, how can you forgive all that?"

God- "Then I sent my Son for nothing."

John 6:63 ...*the words that I speak unto you, they are spirit, and they are life.*

Proverbs 18:21 *Death and life are in the power of the tongue.*

God tells us to speak directly to our problems and not to God about the problem. Most of you go to God telling Him everything that is wrong about you. He already knows. He wants you to start taking that power and authority He has given you and start exercising it through your words.

Mark 11:23 ...*Speak to the mountain.*

If sickness is my mountain, speak to it. God has given us His power. Words release the power. It is His power living inside of me. 'It's not ME!' Many people are still speaking to God about their mountain. He told us to speak to the mountain.

Titus 2:1 *But speak thou the things which become sound doctrine:*

If we speak life, we get life, if we speak death, we get death. If we speak things over ourselves or over others such as, "You will probably have cancer just like your father or mother did," this is speaking death over yourself or over someone else. There are so many words that we speak in a day that can either bring life or death to us or those around us. "You are always sick." "The flu is going around; I'll probably get it." You hear these things around you in the world often. God says, what you speak affects your body. The words we speak seem vital to our health and well being. He 'spoke' and the earth was formed, sickness left, and blind eyes were opened by a spoken word from His mouth. Death and life are voice activated. This is another law that God has put into place just like gravity. Learn to speak His language. He gives us direction in His word how to do that. I actually don't like calling them laws. They are promises given to us by God.

It may seem strange when you first begin to speak His truths and not rely on what your physical eyes may see. Your words bring life or death. If what you have been speaking and doing isn't working for you, try doing what God has said and start speaking His language. He tells us to choose life and teaches us about our words. Though you may be speaking to a cold or cancer and you are not seeing healing with your physical eyes or feeling healed, these words of life have given life. Keep standing on truth even if it seems strange to you.

Each day the Lord quickens me to the words that I speak, and I am changing them! I only want to speak His truths, "By His stripes I am healed, I am blessed, with long life will You satisfy me. "

Ps 118:17 *I shall not die, but live, and declare the works of the Lord.*

I speak His Words over me and others.

When I first began confessing with my mouth "By His stripes I am healed," it felt wrong to me, like I was trying to be a God myself. My husband thought I was going to cause lightening to strike from heaven for confessing such things. I think my husband kept his distance for a-while, not wanting to take the strike himself. I had revelations, that I already had it all, by His stripes I was already healed. This helped take me away from the lie that I had to perform and be good enough for God to answer my prayers. He's already done it. He's provided all that I need. We will never be good enough to receive God's healing if it relied on us. The fact is it's already done. I get it. I got it; it's already living inside of me. I need to speak it out.

I am still amazed at the looks I get when I speak 'life.' But when others speak 'death' people don't think twice about it. Even when those who say they believe in all Jesus did, the words they speak and say tell me differently.

One of the keys for me is that everything God is ever going to do, He has already done! He put it all into place already and now He wants us to believe, receive, and act on it. This is difficult for our minds to comprehend at first. Religion teaches that we have to perform and beg God because we are such sinners. Yes, we thank Him for His mercy, because we already have it. Now we need to restore our minds to His truths about this and start speaking forth His truths. We are no longer sinners saved by grace; we are already healed, prosperous, forgiven, and set free! The spoken word helps us believe. It helped to begin to turn my ship and renew my mind to His truths. Speaking aloud still seems to have more power and authority for me. I remember many times raising my hand in the car driving and speaking aloud His truths. People must have thought I was a little weird. But I don't care. I love my Father. I will shout it from street corners and scream it on the mountain tops. I wanted to live. I wanted that awesome life God has for us! I want it for you!

It took many times for me, especially at first, to renew my mind, to get rid of all the unbelief and lies that I had read, been taught, and lived with for so long. I had scriptures all over my home and when a lie would come to my thoughts such as "You will be sick," I would speak out God's truths, "By His stripes I am healed." When I first started believing His truths this happened often, sometimes many times in a minute. I just kept speaking God's truths aloud to renew my mind and to remind myself of what God's truths were.

Proverbs 18:7 *A fool's mouth is his destruction, and his lips are the snare of his soul.*

Mark 11:23....*For whosoever shall SAY unto this mountain, Be thou removed.......but shall believe that those things which he saith shall come to pass: he shall have whatsoever he saith.*

Proverbs 18: 20, 21 *Death and life are in the power of the tongue;*

God has much to say about the words we speak, and how they affect our health and other matters in our life. Speaking God's word helps us to counter the things that we have learned that come against His truths.

Romans 12:2 *Be transformed, changed by the total renewal of your mind.*

We need to think like God, not the Enemy, the world or religion. The Enemy and the world would have us believe that sickness is just a part of today's life, that we are going to experience the exact same things the world will have to experience, such as poverty, tornados, sickness, and disease.

You hear people say, "We all have to die of something." People say you cannot escape the consequences of living in a fallen polluted world. These are all lies, if you listen to the world around you and focus on these things and that is what you believe then that is what you will then get! What is it that we do get as believers? The previous chapter contains the list of wonderful things that are ours. Things will try to come against us and this is when we need to start using the power of words. God says, "No weapon formed against us shall prosper." Weapons will come against us, but we have the power to defeat them with our words.

The spoken word of God imparts Spirit life into your physical body. The spoken word can change the cells in your body.

John 6:63 *It is the spirit that quickeneth; the flesh profiteth nothing: the words that I speak unto you, they are spirit, and they are life.*

His word is incorruptible seed, and it produces after its kind.

1 Peter 1:23 *Being born again, not of corruptible seed, but of incorruptible, by the word of God, which liveth and abideth for ever.*

There will always be someone who will challenge you and say you are speaking lies if you say something like, "I am blessed" even though there is evidence still of sickness on you. God's word becomes grafted into your body as you speak His truths. You do not deny that sickness exists, but you deny its right to exist in your body, you have been redeemed from the curse of the law and delivered from the authority of darkness.

Galatians 3:13 *Christ hath redeemed us from the curse of the law, being made a curse for us: for it is written, Cursed is every one that hangeth on a tree:*

Col. 1:13. *Who hath delivered us from the power of darkness, and hath translated us into the kingdom of his dear Son:*

In Deuteronomy chapters 28 and 29, God talks about blessings and cursings. The curses are sickness and disease and He says He has delivered us from them. He hasn't delivered us from the blessings. He has left us with ALL the blessings. What an awesome God we have! I certainly don't deserve the blessings that were gifted to us through the death of His Son, but as a believer I get them all! So do you, IF YOU BELIEVE. This is for everyone, believers and non believers. He continually pours out His love for us. He gave it all to us at the cross with His Son, Jesus. It is ours for the taking. Saved - SOZO - healed, prosperous, forgiven, and set free. If you can remember and believe all that He did at the cross, it will help you receive from Him the blessings, not just going to heaven when you die, but heaven right here on earth. Change the language you speak to His language. One of the things God says we have is power and authority. Your voice is your authority. You need to know His truths so that you can begin to thank Him and receive them.

Proverbs 18: 20, 21 *Death and life are in the power of the tongue.*

I hear many teachers say we need to re-visit all the curses of our ancestors in order to be delivered from them. It's the truth that sets you free. The truth is that your ancestors are not a factor for your life and freedom. God is your answer and is what will release the power for you to be set free, not visiting all the demons, curses, and junk from your past. It's knowing the truth, the truth of Jesus Christ and His incredible love. The truth that your parents had a certain bent towards abuse, does not make you an abuser, knowing this truth actually brings freedom. The truth is you now have a new life in Christ Jesus. He loves you so much. His desire is for freedoms in your life. If abuse is a mountain, speak to it. Abuse does not have to hold you in bondage any longer. You can be free from it. If addictions are your mountain, set your focus on Jesus and all His promises and they will no longer have control of you. Speak to them.

Denying sickness won't make you well. However by mixing your faith, the faith of Jesus Christ, and your belief with God's word (His truths) you are calling for the promise of God to be manifest in your body, all His promises. Speak to the mountain. This is not the power of positive thinking; this is just simply stating a fact, the fact of what has already been given to us.

Ephesians 6:13 *Wherefore take unto you the whole armor of God, that ye may be able to withstand in the evil day, and having done all, to stand.*

2 Corinthians 10:5 *I demolish arguments and every pretension that sets itself up against the knowledge of God, and I take captive every thought to make it obedient to Christ.*

People will speak negative things and lies of unbelief over us that will negate the healing power of God from operating in our lives if we receive and believe their words. We need to be aware of this. Jesus, while ministering in His own town, could only heal a few because of the unbelief that was there (Mark 8:22-26). Then He countered the unbelief by going around speaking the word, sharing the good news. He didn't give up on the people. He continued to go around in a circuit coming back to the places of unbelief and sharing the truth. We often give up on people after one time of sharing with them. Jesus kept going back. He didn't give up on them. He didn't abandon them in their unbelief; He went around speaking the truth to help them in their unbelief to help them renew their minds to the truth.

Every time I would hear a whisper of a lie from the Enemy or my own thought, I would repeat the truth by saying out loud the following scripture.

2 Corinthians 10:5 *I demolish arguments and every pretension that sets itself up against the knowledge of God, and I take captive every thought to the obedience of Christ.*

I began to recognize the Enemies lies, the lies of the world and of others as well as my own lying thoughts. Our thoughts are often released from our mouth or we often speak our thoughts out loud. I want my thoughts to be His thoughts so that I am releasing life.

When Jesus healed the blind man in Bethsaida, it was one of the two places He said that had more unbelief than any others. He had to take the man by the hand and lead him out of the town. He did this not because He had all this time and wanted to get alone or it was prettier outside the city, Jesus could heal the man the first time but He knew there was unbelief in the town. It takes belief on our part. He needed to get the man away from the unbelieving people in this town so that the man would believe and the unbelief would not hinder his own healing. The man received his healing after Jesus prayed for him two times. Jesus told the man not to return to that place and to not tell anyone there.

We often see people in Church who have been healed, lose their healing because of negative unbelief spoken into their lives. "Were you really healed? Maybe you should go see the doctor and get some medication, chemo, or radiation?" (Luke 10:12-13) Unbelief enters back in where it would hinder and possibly rob his healing. It is said that only 35% of those healed retain their healing. I believe it is just as the blind man would have witnessed, those in Bethsaida would have begun to speak unbelief into his life again bringing doubt and then unbelief, losing his healing. This is often when God is blamed. We need to be aware of the hindrances around us, which include family, friends, church and even Pastors who speak unbelief and lies into our lives. I love them, but they were wrong, and I pray that they come to know His truth.

So here again we see perhaps why many in our churches are not being healed. There seems to be much unbelief among the body of Christ. Many say it is not for this day, or that was the Old Testament. You never know whom God will heal? God has provided all the healing already, now it is our turn to speak life, to heal the sick, and raise the dead. It is our turn and not just a few really religious healing anointed people. All of us!

1 Corinthians 12:30 *Have all the gifts of healing? Do all speak with tongues? Do all interpret?*

Mark16:16-18 *Go ye into all the world, and preach the gospel to every creature. He that believeth and is baptized shall be saved; (sozo) but he that believeth not shall be damned. And these signs shall follow them that believe; In my name shall they cast out devils; they shall speak with new tongues; They shall take up serpents; and if they drink any deadly thing, it shall not hurt them; they shall lay hands on the sick, and they shall recover.*

Luke 10:9 *And heal the sick that are therein, and say unto them, The kingdom of God is come nigh unto you.*

He was speaking to the disciples and now we are His disciples, and He has commanded us to go do the same things. Remember He said we would be doing even greater things.

What is a Disciple? A scholar, sometimes applied to the followers of John the Baptist but principally to the followers of Christ. A disciple of Christ is one who:
Believes his doctrine,
Rests on his sacrifice,
Imbibes his spirit, and
Imitates his example.

God has provided healing and healing power for all who believe – for all His disciples.

Mark 8:22-25 *Then He came to Bethsaida; and they brought a blind man to Him, and begged Him to touch him. So He took the blind man by the hand and led him out of the town. And when He had spit on his eyes and put His hands on him, He asked him if he saw anything. And he looked up and said, "I see men like trees, walking." Then He put [His] hands on his eyes again and made him look up. And he was restored and saw everyone clearly.*

This is one of the few notations where we see Jesus praying two times for someone's healing in scripture. He prayed the first time and then asked the man, "What do you see?" The man replied. "I see men walking as trees" (The man's healing was not complete yet.) Jesus then prayed the second time for the man and asked him, "Now what do you see?" The blind man was now fully restored of his sight. We often abort the miracle before the manifestation has taken place. When we pray and don't see the miracle manifest immediately, we make excuses that have hindered the church by saying things like, "God must need to teach you something," or, "perhaps God does not want to heal you."

Most of us, if we can live without receiving our healing, we will. However, if whatever you have isn't going to kill you, you often will continue in life without believing and receiving your healing." Most of us will not press in if it is not a matter of life and death. So I am doing the pressing in. I am doing the research into His word in hopes that you get it, that you reach out and take hold for ALL that He has for you. I desire that not one of you be lost, lose your life, or live the average Christian life. It's all about His incredible love, the sacrifice of His Son. I want all to be walking in the abundant life He has said we have available to us. Ephesians 3:20. When a person needing healing passes our shadows, they are instantly healed. What an incredible day this will be.

When we are filled with the abundant health, are prosperous and are living the free life, He tells us. We are free from worries and fear, which is when we will really be effectual in sharing the Gospel.

Americans are so used to going to doctors that we believe in them and not in what God says in His word. Instead of studying the word of God, we study all about medicine and sickness, performing online searches about the latest unbelief. Instead, find out what God says.

I believe doctors are here for the un-believers. When my diagnoses was cancer, many said this is now the time for me to get as much knowledge as possible about cancer and read everything I can about it. This sounded right to me. But God told me to "immerse myself in His word." His actual words to me were, "No Connie, Now is the time you need to find out everything I say about healing." I was to read everything He says about sickness and disease, healing and believing, and what He provided for me (a sinner) at the cross. Not what the world says.

I sometimes catch myself today speaking words that do not bring life. For instance, I might say that I have some ailment. However, I have wonderful friends around me that if I don't catch and change my words, they will remind me of what I just spoke and who I am in Christ. I don't deny that I may have a challenge or something trying to come against me, but I don't' speak it out, or I try not to. I try to say, "Yes I may have a challenge today, but my God says, "By His stripes I am healed (past tense) and made whole."

I am amazed at the words from those who say they believe. I will no more finish praying for someone's healing and out of their mouth will come 'death.' Words like, "Well I guess I better go to the doctor. This may kill me." Or something equally as silly. Two seconds prior they had said they believe God has healed them. If God is and has, as I have been sharing, then why go to the doctor? Most people believe God can heal, but are not sure He will heal them. The truth is He has already completely healed everyone He is ever going to. He did it at the cross. We need to understand this and receive it. It is a done deal, people! He's done everything He is ever going to. He doesn't pick and choose, He's not a hit and miss God, you are the one who needs to believe it and receive it.

Others have actually said to me, that it would be a greater testimony of God if I was to go to the doctor and get another diagnosis of cancer and be healed again! Wouldn't it speak greater of my God that I am living in health every day? That I no longer have to rely on a doctor's wisdom for health or healing. I believe He wants us living in health. I don't believe He wants us living from sickness to sickness, or even from miracle to miracle!

When I was diagnosed with cancer in the early days of my believing, I had many people say I needed to have some kind of follow-up treatment, such as chemo, or drugs of some kind. I felt if God had already healed me what reason would I have to do chemo? I so trust in my Jesus that I know that I have health, not just healing. I am health as He is. I will not entertain those thoughts.

Andrew Wommack tells a story of a woman who went through surgery for some form of cancer, and then was healed miraculously through Jesus. Her family was not so convinced and through much persuasion talked her into having radiation treatments. Remember, she was totally healed from the cancer, not by the doctors but through knowing the truth of Jesus Christ and believing. She had a reaction to the radiation and died. You may ask why didn't she get healed from the reaction to the radiation, God had already healed her, her belief must have weakened as she then listened to her family and began to put her trust in the medicines of man. Healing lost!

God has already done everything. He's provided all the healing that He is ever going to do. It was finished at the cross. The woman in Andrew Wommack's story believed for her healing and received it and then was persuaded to unbelief, by the spoken words of those around her. It is amazing how we can be going along great walking in health and a spoken word (death) comes from someone's mouth and we start entertaining those words. We will start thinking maybe there is truth to some of what they are saying, and then we will start feeling certain symptoms associated with that. It is not even what one would call psychosomatic sickness. It is usually something like the flu or cold or something that is going around and we had probably already entertained the thought in our 'thick' heads. When they spoke it, we entertained it even more. Quickly remembering God's truths and His spoken word we can begin to speak life back over ourselves. "By His stripes I am already healed." Amen. My body is programmed to respond to my voice, but I can invite others into my sphere of authority.

Proverbs 18:20-21 *A man's belly shall be satisfied with the fruit of his mouth; and with the increase of his lips shall he be filled. Death and life are in the power of the tongue: and they that love it shall eat the fruit thereof.*

1 Corinthians 14:9-10 *So likewise ye, except ye utter by the tongue words easy to be understood, how shall it be known what is spoken? for ye shall speak into the air. There are, it may be, so many kinds of voices in the world, and none of them is without signification.*

Every part of me is made by the spoken word of God. I am one Spiritual being. It is difficult when we are speaking two different languages to get the body to respond to that spoken word that is foreign to it. A Pastor I know shared a story to illustrate this. When he was in the service he was sent overseas. He spoke to a dog in his language, "Here doggy" and the dog did not respond.

When you can speak to the dog in its own language it will respond and come to you. When we speak to our bodies and our mountains in a language that is foreign to them, they will not respond. We need to know that our cells respond to our words, our language. We need to know the language God speaks, the spiritual laws, and the language our bodies know. "By His stripes I am healed." A vital key to know is that I can speak life into my body or I can speak death. Which do you prefer? I need to know the truth and what God's Spiritual laws are, which are, health, prosperity, freedom, and forgiveness. Speak these life affirming words into your life, around others and into others, but especially into yourself. Again, your body is voice activated.

1 Thes.2:13 *For this cause also thank we God without ceasing, because, when ye received the word of God which ye heard of us, ye received it not as the word of men, but as it is in truth, the word of God, which effectually worketh also in you that believe.*

Lay a strong foundation of Godly speech. Speak life not death. Speak health not sickness, wealth not poverty. This will change your mind. It will renew your mind to the truth and remind you continually of who you truly are in Him. It will change the cells in your body to health. (that is if you are speaking health).

Psalm 19:14 *Let the words of my mouth, and the meditation of my heart, be acceptable in thy sight, O Lord, my strength, and my redeemer.*

Do not be like some who speak and speak and speak and when they pray they have so many words trying to convince themselves and you that God's word is true. They put everyone to sleep. Do not be that clanging cymbal. I used to be that clanging cymbal and that is one reason I know. It's used to try to convince ourselves and others. Be convinced and your words will be fewer!

Matthew 6:7,8 *But when ye pray, use not vain repetitions, as the heathen do: for they think that they shall be heard for their much speaking. Be not ye therefore like unto them: for your Father knoweth what things ye have need of, before ye ask him.*

I used to put a list of reminders on my mirror. I would write scripture promises and notes of what He did for me in the past, what He says in His word, and what I have. I reminded myself that He healed a cold, delivered me from cigarette smoking, brought me my husband…'miracles'… healed me of cancer. Because I was still filled with much unbelief I still needed to continually feed the belief in me by renewing my mind to God's truths daily.

Once it became more a part of me than the unbelief, I no longer had to have as many notes to remind me of His truths. I still read His word daily and remind myself in this way. I sometimes need to have more notes! The world is so filled with the unbelief of spoken negative unbelieving words, that we need to counter them with His truths.

I made a brochure of Healing Scriptures that are a quick reference for me to look at and read.   I give them to anyone who wants to change. They are His words and promises to us. It is a great tool to have with me and read over myself as I believe for the manifestation of something to come. I speak them out loud. The power of the spoken word heals the sick, raises the dead, opens blind eyes, restores marriages, and looks to a God who has provided everything for us through His incredible love.   But I am amazed at those who say they want healing but are not even willing to read one scripture, even if I have written them all down.

Ephesians 6:20 *For which I am an ambassador in bonds: that therein I may speak boldly, as I ought to speak.*

I will tell everyone who wants to listen about this incredible Jesus I know. I will be His ambassador. I wish that all would be speaking boldly of His great love and grace and the power and authority that are ours for the taking. Read the word and believe it! Then speak it aloud to yourself, your family, friends and all who will hear. There is life and death in your tongue and in your spoken words. Speak life!

Prayer:
"I Keep asking that YOU, the God of my Lord Jesus Christ, my glorious Father, that YOU give me the spirit of wisdom and revelation so I may know You better. I pray also that the eyes of my heart may be enlightened in order that I may know the hope to which You have called me, the glorious inheritance to me and Your incomparably great power for me ---who believes... Ephesians 1:17-19. Thank you Lord for your truths and that the words of my mouth speak only your truths.
Amen

Additional scripture references.

Proverbs 21: 23 *Whoso keepeth his mouth and his tongue keepeth his soul from troubles.*

Proverbs 10:11 *The mouth of a righteous man is a well of life.*

Proverbs 12:6 ...*The mouth of the upright shall deliver*

them.

Proverbs 12:14 *A man shall be satisfied with good by the fruit of his mouth.*

Proverbs 12:18 ...*The tongue of the wise is health.*

Proverbs 13:3 *He that keepeth his mouth keepeth his life.*

Proverbs 14:3..*the lips of the wise shall preserve them.*

Proverbs 15:4 *A wholesome tongue is a tree of life....*

Proverbs 15:4 *A gentle tongue is a tree of life, but...*

Proverbs 15:2 *The tongue of the wise useth knowledge aright.*

Proverbs 16:24 *Pleasant words are as a honeycomb, sweet to the soul, and health to the bones.*

Mark 16:17 *And these signs shall follow them that believe; In my name shall they cast out devils; they shall speak with new tongues;*

1 Peter 4:11 *If any man speak, let him speak as the oracles of God; if any man minister, let him do it as of*

the ability which God giveth: that God in all things may be glorified through Jesus Christ, to whom be praise and dominion for ever and ever. Amen.

Chapter 7

The Lies and Deception of Satan

The Enemy has been given too much power and authority in our lives as believers. I personally have given it to him, by default, by lack of understanding, and through deception and lies.

The only thing the Enemy has is lies and deception. He has NO power over us. He does exist, and we personally give him power, through believing the lies and deception. Outside of that he is nothing and has no power.

Where are lies and deception conceived? In our minds! This is where the Enemy has been battling, and this is where I have engaged in his battle for way too long. A friend once said, "As long as I engage in the battle, the battle will wage." It takes time to disengage from this battle. We are told as Christians we must 'battle the enemy.' And yes, we must. I have been battling with the wrong strategy, and with the wrong weapons. God says "the weapons of our warfare, are not the weapons of the world, on the contrary they have divine power to demolish strongholds."

2 Corinthians 10:4 *(For the weapons of our warfare are not carnal, but mighty through God to the pulling down of strong holds ;)*

God wants us to prepare our minds for action. He wants us to be 'single-minded,' and focused on the things of God, not the world, or workings of the Enemy. He wants us to look to Him and His truths.

2 Corinthians 10: 3-4... vs. 7 says... *you are looking only on the surface of things.*

Col 3:2 *'Set our minds on things above.* HE is our *things above*, our promises and provision are the things to set our minds on.

1 Sam. 17:47 *Do not be afraid or discouraged. ... the battle is the Lord's.*

2 Chronicles 20:15 ...*The battle is not yours but God's.*

2 Corinthians 10:5 *I demolish arguments and every pretension that sets itself up against the knowledge of God, and I take captive every thought to make it obedient to Christ.*

We now have the mind of Christ; it is His power working in us.

From the very beginning Satan has used his lies and deception to get us to believe that the truths of God are not for everyone, or that God's words are misinterpreted. He came as a serpent to Adam and Eve and deceived Eve to believing lies and she began to doubt and think that perhaps the things God had spoken were not true, and unbelief began to enter in. Satan asked Eve, "Did God really say?" Gen. 3:1-6 Did God really say that eating of the tree of good and evil would kill you? He asked a question that made them question what God's truth was. Satan still does this today when people say things like, "Does God really heal? Are you not learning through being sick?" These are some of the lies being spread that Satan just loves to have God's people repeat.

Eve's mind was now focused on what the Enemy planted and not on all the wonderful things of God. Amazing how we can still have a thousand wonderful things from God and one little question or statement will have us question the very character of God. That is why I used to put up scriptures and write on sticky notes and put them on my mirror where I would see them to remind myself what my Jesus say's.

We need to know God's character. He is a good God. Our God is patient, loving, kind and filled with goodness, compassion, grace and mercy. He's not striking us with disease.

Satan will mix a little truth with his lies. He is the great deceiver. He leads the whole world astray. Rev. 12:9. Eve was deceived by the serpent's cunning. Eve's focus was no longer on the Lord and His truths; she was now looking at and contemplating the things Satan had lied to her about. The same happened to Adam also, as he ate of the fruit too and was right there when Satan was using his lies and deception.

2 Corinthians 11:3 *But I fear, lest by any means, as the serpent beguiled Eve through his subtilty, so your minds should be corrupted from the simplicity that is in Christ.*

Even Paul's thorn in the flesh is used to deceive us. In 2 Corinthians 12:6-10 We read that the thorn was a messenger of Satan to buffet him - lest he should be exalted above measure. There is no place that says it is sickness or a disease or an eye affliction as we have been told by so many. It was not given to him by God but was a 'messenger from Satan, to buffet him.' Paul's thorn was people, not sickness.

I do not like to spend much time discussing the Enemy and his deceptive ways, but it needs to be addressed. Knowing the truth about the Enemy is one of the things that was very freeing for me from receiving his lies and deception. God says the truth will set you free.

John 8:32 *And ye shall know the truth, and the truth shall make you free.*

Knowing His truth, I mean really knowing the truth, sets me free. Knowing who God is, is what I want to set my heart on and what I want to study. It is like the bankers who study money. They spend hours looking at the real thing and when the counterfeit comes they recognize it right away. It is the same with our precious Jesus, our Lord. Study Him and get to know Him, know His character, how He ministered, what He did, and then when the Enemy's lies and deception come, we can recognize it.

We can counter Satan's lies with the truth of God's word. But I need to know God's truths to counter Satan's lies. Adam and Eve met with God every day. He came and met with them in the garden daily. Adam and Eve had no worldly teachings, no religious Pharisees, or religious traditions. But even they, who knew no evil, or sin, were tempted by Satan, if they were deceived by him, how much more are we susceptible to his lies and deception? If we are trusting God, we must trust in what He says in His word. His Word never changes, He never changes. It takes time to get to know Him. He is a loving God, filled with grace.

Isaiah 26:3 *Thou wilt keep him in perfect peace, whose mind is stayed on thee: because he trusteth in thee.*

The good news is that Jesus came, He died for us, and He left us His Holy Spirit, the comforter. How can we trust someone when we know little about them and never take the time to do so?

Rev. 12:11 *"I overcome Satan by the blood of the lamb and the WORD of my testimony."*

Jesus is my final word. He is my life, everything to me. As I study to know Him and ask Him for revelation and wisdom, I want to understand His love for us more. It is one thing to read the Word of God, it is another thing to believe what God says. READ THE WORD AND BELIEVE IT. DARE TO BELIEVE GOD until the life of Jesus is implanted within your soul.

Be willing to go deeper and dig for gold.

Sin has no more dominion over you. You reign in Christ, and you make rightful use of His finished work. Don't moan and travail for a week. If you are in need, "only believe" (Mark 5:36). Don't fast to get some special thing, "only believe". "Have faith in God" (Mark 11:22) If you are free in God, Believe! Believe and it will be unto you even as you believe. (Mt 9:29) (Taken from: Smith Wigglesworth's Daily Devotional).

I believe we should pray and fast, I believe it is for us, to change us, to get our thoughts so focused on our Lord that our minds are stayed on Him. It is absolutely not to change God! I see many who are praying and fasting to 'get' God to change some situation in their or someone's life. God cannot change. He is the same; yesterday, today and forever. We can change by renewing our minds to God's truths. This can be accomplished when we pray and fast. It disciplines our bodies to know that we are not going to die after a few hours without food. We are not going to die every time we feel a pain.

Hebrews 13:8 *Jesus Christ the same yesterday, and today, and forever.*

2 Peter 1:3. *His divine power has given to us all things that pertain to life and godliness, through knowledge of Him who call us by glory and virtue.*

God has given us greater authority. We are deflated when we give that authority to Satan.

Ephesians 3:20 *Now unto him that is able to do exceeding abundantly above all that we ask or think, according to the power that worketh in us.*

Remind Satan of who and what Jesus gave to you. Believe what God gave to you and not the lies of Satan or the lies of the world.

John 10:10 *The thief cometh not, but for to steal, and to kill, and to destroy: I am come that they might have life, and that they might have it more abundantly.*

When you hear the enemy's lies whispering in your ear. "Is this what God really says?" Counter those lies with scriptures. My God says, and then quote Jesus. Such as 1 Peter 2:24 "By His stripes I am healed." We have all entertained his lies in the past, we can become more aware of Satan's lies as we study God's truths, and then when we hear the Enemy whisper his lies we can counter with the truth of God.

James 4:7 *Submit yourselves to God, resist the devil and he will flee from you.*

God instructs us to 'resist' the devil. Become pro active in your battle. There would be no resisting to be done, if we had not heard a lie, or been sent a wrong message, there needs to be 'something' to resist. Hearing from Satan is not a sin; however God wants us to be more aware of Satan's lies and deception and to resist Satan. He wants us to be so close to Him, that we recognize the Enemy when he does come and whisper a lie to us.

I heard the Enemy whisper to me when I was writing in this chapter about Paul's thorn, Satan said, "Not all sickness is demonic. This world is polluted. There are other reasons for sickness, disease, and death." (Again, some truth mixed with his lies.) I entertained it for a moment, when I realized this was a 'lie' from Satan. I countered with the word of God. For my God says, Mark 16:18 "I can drink deadly poison and it will not harm me." Psalm 91:16 "With long life will He satisfy me." 1 Peter 2:24"By HIS stripes, I am healed…." Every time I hear a lie, I try to counter with the truth. Do I always recognize Satan's lies? No, but again as I study the real thing (God's truths) I sure recognize the Enemy's lies much quicker than I used to.

Prayer:
Lord thank You for Your wisdom and understanding and that I recognize the lies of the enemy. Amen.

Let us all know Him more. Let us all know His love. What an incredible gift. How marvelous to see that our Savior, born to a virgin, would give His life for us. He came to give us life and more abundantly, to set the 'captives' free, to bring Salvation. He was being prepared for those first 32 years of His life, to become a mighty Savior to the world. How incredibly awesome is that! Do we think that we do not need to prepare ourselves to be His voice to the world?

I have been accused of using the words awesome and blessed too much, but I cannot think of words that would describe my Savior any better than these. How much love He has for each of us, and how much love the Father has for us that He would 'give' His only Son to suffer and die for us so that we do not have to. The Enemy wants us to believe that we are to suffer and die all over again, and again, and again. As Mary said.. "Be it unto me, according to Your Word."

Psalm 118:17 *I will not die but live and declare the works of God. I am the temple of the Holy Spirit, "Lord I place my confidence in you."*

When the Enemy comes at you with a lie it could be a whisper, a word from a doctor, a pain in your side, or finances. It is easier for me if I counter that lie immediately with God's truth. One thing I have learned is that if I entertain those lies, it is a little harder for me to come against them. If I recognize the Enemy's tactics and lies quickly, I can speak God's word and truth into that situation, whether again it's a pain in my side or finances. I speak to that mountain.

Matthew 17:20 *And Jesus said unto them, Because of your unbelief: for verily I say unto you, If ye have faith as a grain of mustard seed, ye shall say unto this mountain, Remove hence to yonder place; and it shall remove; and nothing shall be impossible unto you.*

The moment a pain comes into my body, if I speak to it that instant it usually goes away just as fast as it came. I try to not let the thoughts of sickness or other things become a lingering thought. The battle will not wage as long as I do not engage in Satan's lies! I am not always successful at putting the thoughts away and I end up engaging in them.

I had struggled with migraines for years, every time I had a certain thing happen such as a knot in the base of my neck, in the past this meant I would get the migraine. It has taken me a while for this to be overcome because of the lies of Satan, because of my own thoughts. I now have much more success in this area of my life for when I first feel a knot, I begin to say "No, by His stripes I am already healed. I command this knot to go I speak to the vessels and veins in my head and neck. Migraine's are a thing of the past." On occasion I entertain the thoughts for too long and then it takes longer for me to overcome. But I have more victory now! WOOO HOO!

I recently recognized that I had been working way too many hours and was in need of a little time for my body to rest. I began to feel the symptoms of a migraine, and my husband asked me if I was speaking to that symptom. I recognized right away that I was not. I needed some time off, and a migraine meant I would get some 'rest' even if was not a fun rest. I then began to speak to the pain, and it took a little while nearly five hours, but the pain then subsided. I still consider this a victory. I ended up with a bad headache, but it never went into a migraine. He reminds me I could get rest without being flat on my back with a migraine. So speak to those mountains the moment they arise. Use the power and authority that Jesus has given us and stop listening to the lies and deception of the Enemy whose only goal is to steal, kill, and destroy you.

The enemy continues to try to come against us with symptoms. Sometimes they are natural, either way I have a way out. His Name is Jesus Christ.

I grew up as a gymnast and recently wanted to see how I faired at doing a simple cartwheel in our backyard. When I put my first hand down, with my new found weight that I have acquired, I felt the bones in my hand

and wrist crunch under me and excruciating pain. Instead of going to that 'uh oh' place I used to go to, I immediately placed my hand over my other and spoke to the pain, telling it to leave. I spoke to every joint and bone commanding them to be healthy and healed. In the name of Jesus. The pain left and I went about my evening forgetting all about the incident. When I awoke the next morning, my hand and wrist were purple and swollen and the same excruciating pain had returned. I simply put my hand over it again and spoke to the pain and the bruising commanding it to go. I also spoke in tongues. Within moments the pain stopped and I took my hand from under the covers and the bruising and swelling were now gone also.

I shared this with my husband later, and he asked me why I had not told him about it at the time. Now, I love my husband, he has been healed himself, but he still has a tendency to go to that place of unbelief at times. I didn't tell him because I knew he would probably speak that unbelief to me, and I would need to come against his words. It is much easier for me to take care of these things without engaging others, especially if they still have unbelief. I have enough of my own at times!

Prayer:
"Lord, we command the lies and deception of Satan to be

removed from our thoughts and lives. Thank you for renewing our minds to your truths."

Amen

Additional scripture references

1 Peter 2:24 *Who his own self bare our sins in his own body on the tree, that we, being dead to sins, should live unto righteousness: by whose stripes ye were healed.*

Isaiah 54:17 *No weapon that is formed against thee shall prosper; and every tongue that shall rise against thee in judgment thou shalt condemn. This is the heritage of the servants of the Lord, and their righteousness is of me, saith the Lord.*

Ephesians 3:21 *To Him be the glory in the Church by Christ Jesus to all generations, forever and ever. Amen*

John 8:32 *And ye shall know the truth, and the truth shall make you free.*

Forever Changed

Chapter 8
Trials, Testings and Tribulations

We are often told by religion that we will face trials and tribulations and, that these are put upon us by God Himself to train us, and to teach us a lesson." We are told that God loves us so much that He will give us cancer to help us grow. Who would want to serve this God? No wonder the world looks upon us as if we are nuts at times. Who in their right mind would follow after a God who gives people cancer, sickness and disease? Who would follow a God who strikes your child with Leukemia, and kills a mother with four young children, so that someone else may learn a lesson or come to know this God? I, for one, would not want anything to do with this kind of God, and I don't think most of the world would either. This is evidenced by the number of people who are giving their lives to Him these days.

How many of you have really thanked God for a family member dying young because it taught you a lesson? First, God did not kill that family member; He's in the business of life, not death. Death is from Satan, that's his job. So do you thank Satan?

We have given our Lord a bad name by spouting these lies. I have even spouted them myself in the past! I couldn't explain that a friend's baby died when we all believed he would survive. When we don't always have the answer, we tend to blame God. We have spoken such words as, "You never know what God has planned through this tragedy." I have heard people say, "This is one of the greatest mysteries of God, we never know who He is going to heal and who He chooses to let die." My God is not schizophrenic. He is not the one who brings sickness and disease, He is not mysterious. He has a much greater plan for peoples' lives.

Never take my word as gospel, check it with the word of God. Let the word of God get in the way of your religion, and your beliefs.

Let's look at the scriptures so often used incorrectly to tell us that God gives us sickness, disease and accidents to teach us, or to save another person.

Proverbs 3:11,12, *My son, do not despise the Lord's discipline and do not resent His rebuke, because the Lord disciplines those He loves, as a father the son he delights in.*

Deuteronomy 24:5,6 *Know then in your heart that as a man disciplines his son, so the LORD your God disciplines you.*

Hebrews 12:3-12 *Consider him who endured such opposition from sinful men, so that you will not grow weary and lose heart. In your struggle against sin, you have not yet resisted to the point of shedding your blood. And you have forgotten that word of encouragement that addressed you as sons: "My son, do not make light of the Lord's discipline, and do not lose heart when he rebukes you, because the Lord disciplines those he loves, and he punishes everyone he accepts as a son. Finding hardship as discipline; God is treating you as sons; For what son is not disciplined by his father?*

If you are not disciplined (and everyone undergoes discipline) then you are illegitimate children and not true sons. Moreover, we have all had human fathers who disciplined us and we respected them for it.

God didn't give us sickness nor does He kill us to teach us a lesson or to teach someone else a lesson. Yet there is a discipline that seems to be evident in His word. He gave us His words to teach us. Does sickness or death make you holy? No, what is it that makes you holy?"

Romans 6:22 *But now being made free from sin, and become servants to God, ye have your fruit unto holiness, and the end everlasting life.*

The mere fact that we now believe in Christ and serve Him is what makes us holy. It is His holiness living inside of us. None of us on our own are holy.

The meaning of the word discipline is to punish, guide, instruct, provide guidance.

How do you discipline your son? Do you beat him? Do you give him cancer? Do you guide him off a bridge? Break his arm? Maybe! Then I should report you to child protective services. The police should be notified.

A loving Father shares the truth with his children. Through the understanding of that truth, change can take place. Remember it's the truth that sets people free, free from sickness, strife, disease, depression, and anything else that may try to come against you. You have the power of the living God inside of you to stand against all of those things. The loving Father in Heaven wants you to be living this awesome life here and now. Not in the here after only.

2 Tim 3:14-17 *But continue thou in the things which thou hast learned and hast been assured of, knowing of whom thou hast learned them; And that from a child thou hast known the holy scriptures, which are able to make thee wise unto salvation through faith which is in Christ Jesus. All scripture is given by inspiration of God, and is profitable for doctrine, for reproof, for correction, for instruction in righteousness: That the man of God may be perfect, thoroughly furnished unto all good works.*

In the first covenant with His people, God did chastise and even killed his people. This was 'before' He sent His Son to take away the sins of the world.

John 3:16 *For God so loved the world, that he gave his only begotten Son, that whosoever believeth in him should not perish, but have everlasting life.*

His everlasting life is for today and not just when we all get to Heaven. We now have Heaven on earth. Our earth is our body. Not that we won't be rejoicing in Heaven, I will, we should be rejoicing now! It is heaven to serve the Lord. Everlasting life is now. Again it is not just the hereafter. The Old Covenant is replaced by a new because of the sacrifice of Jesus Christ. This New Covenant is one of grace and love. He paid the price for us to have life, and more abundantly, not in sickness and poverty.

God gave authority over the world to man. Adam was the first man given that power and authority.

Genesis 1:28 *And God blessed them, and God said unto them, Be fruitful, and multiply, and replenish the earth, and subdue it: and have dominion over the fish of the sea, and over the fowl of the air, and over every living thing that moveth upon the earth.*

Have you ever thought why God came to the earth in the form of a man, His Son? He had to become a 'man' in the flesh because that is who He gave the authority to! He could not break His own covenant. He could have just spoken the word and pronounced that now our sins were forgiven and pronounced a 'New Covenant.' But He needed to be flesh a 'man' to accomplish the work. He again would not break His own word. He had given that authority to man, the first Adam. His Son, 'the second Adam,' had to come and declare to the world the truths once again, thus declaring the New Covenant. We no longer are held by our sins, we only need believe.

John 3:18 *He that believeth on him is not condemned: but he that believeth not is condemned already, because he hath not believed in the name of the only begotten Son of God.*

We are no longer under the law for He fulfilled the law.

Romans 7:6 *But now we are delivered from the law, that being dead wherein we were held; that we should serve in newness of spirit, and not in the oldness of the letter.*

Ephesians 2:15-18 *Having abolished in his flesh the enmity, even the law of commandments contained in ordinances; for to make in himself of twain one new man, so making peace; And that he might reconcile both unto God in one body by the cross, having slain the enmity thereby: And came and preached peace to you which were afar off, and to them that were nigh. For through him we both have access by one Spirit unto the Father.*

Most Christians and religious people have it in their heads that 'If they love God enough or do enough good, He will love them and then, they'll be righteous and holy. It is our love of Him that helps us to live righteous, holy lives. We are not holy because of what we do, but because of who He is. It is all about what He did for us, not what we can do for Him. We are not going to Hell because of our sins. We will only go to hell because of our un-belief.

Hebrews 3:19 *So we see that they could not enter in because of unbelief.*

When we sin, it keeps us from living the full, fulfilled, and awesome life God has for us, lives filled with love, joy, peace, prosperity and self-control. We are living in the flesh when we are sinning continually, but we are not going to hell because of our sins. When we are 'single-minded,' having our thoughts on Him and not on the world, this keeps us in peace, joy and love.

Demonic powers are not the driving force behind our sin, though we can give Satan power in our lives when we do sin. Demonic powers have already been stripped of their authority by the Son of God. Remember, Satan is the great deceiver. All Satan has is lies and deception.

In Acts 18 and 19 Paul didn't pray and intercede, He preached the Gospel fearlessly. He took the power of God and preached the truth. People began to turn away from their pagan ways. The truth is the power that overcomes sin, darkness, and Satan -- the true Gospel of Jesus Christ. It is not sickness and disease that teaches lessons so we can live free, grow in our faith, or become better Christians.

John 8:32 *And ye shall know the truth, and the truth shall make you free.*

'The truth sets people free,' not sickness and disease, or trials and testings! Jesus did the intercession for us; we don't need to add anything to His finished work. Anything we add to what Jesus did is denying what He did. We can take the authority and the power He's given us, and stop rejecting the gift of Jesus and His sacrifice on the cross.

We can't ask God to do what He told us to do. Some people are praying and asking God to take away their sickness, cancer, torment and other challenges. If you believe God gave it to you, then this is 'double-mindedness' in a way. Why would you ask God to remove something you believe He gave you to test you with or to try you? He told us to heal the sick and raise the dead.

Mathew 10:1 *And when he had called unto him his twelve disciples, he gave them power against unclean spirits, to cast them out, and to heal all manner of sickness and all manner of disease.*

We are to take our authority and command what God has done to come into place. He gave us the authority and power over all demons. He gave me power and authority to drive out demons and heal every disease and sickness! If the sickness is demonic, cast it out - if it is natural or worldly, cast it out - if it is an accident, command healing to come forth. It is not me doing these things, but rather it is God in me! It's me taking His authority and power given to me and exercising it!

Luke 10:8-9 tells, *Whatever city you enter, and they receive you, eat such things as are set before you, And Heal the sick.*

Matthew 10:8 *Heal the sick, cleanse the lepers, raise the dead, cast out devils: freely ye have received, freely give*

The definition of affliction does not contain the words sickness or disease. It does, however, make reference to people (to crowd). Affliction in the concordance is Thlibo = to crowd, afflict, narrow, throng, suffer tribulation, trouble, anguish, burdened, persecution, tribulation, trouble. Crowds are not sickness and diseases. People are usually the root of affliction in our lives. How many times are we tempted in a day to take offense by a person or group of persons? We are usually tempted to sin because of the influence of people in our lives. The Disciples were persecuted, tried, and afflicted by people. Even as Jesus suffered persecution from people so will we. Jesus' trials, testings, and persecutions were never sickness and disease or accidents.

John 15:18-20 (NIV) *"If the world hates you, keep in mind that it hated me first. If you belonged to the world, it would love you as its own... Remember the words I spoke to you; 'No servant is greater than his master.' If they persecuted me, they will persecute you also."*

2 Corinthians 8:2 *How that in a great trial of affliction the abundance of their joy and their deep poverty abounded unto the riches of their liberality.*

1 Peter 4:12-16 *Beloved, think it not strange concerning the fiery trial which is to try you, as though some strange thing happened unto you: But rejoice, inasmuch as ye are partakers of Christ's sufferings; that, when his glory shall be revealed, ye may be glad also with exceeding joy. If ye be reproached for the name of Christ, happy are ye; for the spirit of glory and of God resteth upon you: on their part he is evil spoken of, but on your part he is glorified. But let none of you suffer as a murderer, or as a thief, or as an evildoer, or as a busybody in other men's matters. Yet if any man suffer as a Christian, let him not be ashamed; but let him glorify God on this behalf.*

The Bible says trials are to be expected. The trial seems to be reproach, which means criticism, accusation, and scolding, rebuke, for being a follower of Jesus Christ. These trials may even be the beatings of men, but again, not sickness and disease.

Even when sickness has come upon us, it does not say to take it and learn from it, that God gave it to us. He tells us IF any of you are sick, to get prayer and be healed! But the word IF here implies His intentions are not for believers to be sick. His intentions are for health and prosperity, forgiveness and freedom… saved!

We can use these afflictions from other people to help us learn and grow. I hope you are starting to get the true meaning of trials, testings, and tribulations. It has been taught in many churches that we are to suffer and be tested with sickness and disease brought on by God and that is how we are to grow in our 'faith.' It may take you some time to renew your minds to the truth of God's word. Don't settle for anything less than His truths. God's best.

1Thes 3:1-4 *Wherefore when we could no longer forbear, we thought it good to be left at Athens alone; And sent Timotheus, our brother, and minister of God, and our fellowlabourer in the gospel of Christ, to establish you, and to comfort you concerning your faith: That no man should be moved by these afflictions: for yourselves know that we are appointed thereunto. For verily, when we were with you, we told you before that we should suffer tribulation; even as it came to pass, and ye know.*

I keep searching for signs that afflictions and tribulations were sickness and disease. The signs were not there; instead it was the people in their lives who were causing trouble. Yes, I agree that before Jesus paid the price there were signs of disease and afflictions brought on by God but that is no longer true, not since He sent His Son to pay the price.

1 Thes 3:6-8 *But now when Timotheus came from you unto us, and brought us good tidings of your faith and charity, and that ye have good remembrance of us always, desiring greatly to see us, as we also to see you: Therefore, brethren, we were comforted over you in all our affliction and distress by your faith: For now we live, if ye stand fast in the Lord.*

In 1 Peter 5:9 the word afflictions is Karos and is defined as worthless, effects, depraved, injurious, bad, evil, harm, ill, noisome, and wicked.

"I Am the Lord who heals you." If our Lord heals us, why would He inflict upon us sickness and disease or hurts and trials in a way that would cause injury or death and then have to get you healed? Perhaps the "testing, trials and tribulations," the troubles in our life -- are people, not sickness and disease? Are you beginning to understand this. It is a huge misconception in the church today.

James 5:14-15 *If any of you is sick, call on the elders, have then lay hands on you, anoint you and pray, and the prayer offered up in faith will heal the sick.*

If you are sick, your job is to call upon the elders, (anyone who's walked longer than you who believe) their part is to anoint you and pray in faith believing, not hoping, (wishful thinking). I no longer pray merely hoping. I pray believing and when I don't see healings manifest I am surprised. I also have the authority in me to heal. Most of the time I don't need to go to the elders because I am one, and I have the power of the living God inside me to heal. There are times where I feel weak and ask those who believe to pray, to command the things to leave and to stand in agreement with me that I am already healed. God tells us to "speak to the mountains." He has given us the power and authority over all sickness and devils.

You can rest assured God will raise you up if you believe. It is the word of God. Many turn away from the Lord for healing. Look at King Asa, who "in his disease...did not seek the Lord." (2 Chron. 16:12-13) Consequently he died. Even if sin had been the cause of his sickness God's word declares in James 5:15, "if he has committed sins, they shall be forgiven." It doesn't even say the person has to repent (as we know it today) but their job was to 'go' to the elders for prayer. One of the by-products of this faith and belief was that if they had sinned, their sins were forgiven. It takes belief on our part to even go to the elders for prayer. That is one step of the faith, our display and exhibiting of our belief. I am not saying we should not repent of sins, but we should turn from our old sinful ways and ask God to forgive us. Remember, He already paid the price for all of our sins.

Mt. 8:8 *"Only speak a Word and my servant shall be healed.*

Eph. 6:11 *Put on the whole armor of God.*

Few who are saved have a right conception of how great their authority is over darkness, sickness, demons, death and every lie of the Enemy. It is a real joy when we realize our inheritance! I spoke at a Christian gathering about our inheritance, and I am amazed at how many 'Christian believers' do not have a right conception of who they are and what they have as an inheritance as a 'believer' in Jesus Christ. We are one with Him, bone of His bone, flesh of His flesh. We have the same DNA, we are members (bone and flesh) with Him.

Ephesians 1:11 *In whom also we have obtained an inheritance, being predestinated according to the purpose of him who worketh all things after the counsel of his own will:*

Ephesians 1:18 *The eyes of your understanding being enlightened; that ye may know what is the hope of his calling, and what the riches of the glory of his inheritance in the saints.*

The definition of Testing is; to examine in order to determine quality, value or character.

1 Peter 4:12 *Beloved, think it not strange concerning the fiery trial which is to try you, as though some strange thing happened unto you*

1 Thes. 2:4 *But as we were allowed of God to be put in trust with the gospel, even so we speak; not as pleasing men, but God, which trieth our hearts.*

Testing is an exam; it is not a sickness or disease or accident. It is our hearts that He is looking at to examine. Are we double minded? What is your character like? Do you have the same character as Jesus Christ? We should. Seldom do I look like Him. But I am on my way. The more I know about who I am the more I begin to look and act like Him.

God testing his people as we see testing through death and persecutions of other kinds is Old Covenant. We now have Jesus. Amen. We are no longer under the Old Covenant; we now have a new life in Jesus Christ, so take it! We have already passed the exam, not by anything we have done, but because of what HE DID. This kind of sounds like cheating! But it is the free gift of Jesus. He is the one who did it all for us. We get to partake now in this glorious accomplishment. I believe Him. I so desire that believers believe Him, too.

As Christians we can 'fight' against temptations - temptations brought on by our own beliefs -- lies of the Enemy and wrong teachings.
By training our selves in Godliness. (Read the word)
Resisting the pressures of the world. (Believe the word)
Continuing consistently in the truth. (Receive the word)
Learning more of God through the scriptures. (Read the word some more)
Giving ourselves wholeheartedly to whatever God has entrusted to us. (Do the word)

2 Thes. 2:14-15 *For ye, brethren, became followers of the churches of God which in Judaea are in Christ Jesus: for ye also have suffered like things of your own*

countrymen, even as they have of the Jews: Who both killed the Lord Jesus, and their own prophets, and have persecuted us; and they please not God, and are contrary to all men:...

1 Tim. 4:7-15 *But refuse profane and old wives' fables, and exercise thyself rather unto godliness. For bodily exercise profiteth little: but godliness is profitable unto all things, having promise of the life that now is, and of that which is to come. This is a faithful saying and worthy of all acceptation. For therefore we both labour and suffer reproach, (a mild rebuke or criticism) because we trust in the living God, who is the Savior of all men, specially of those that believe. These things command and teach. Let no man despise thy youth; but be thou an example of the believers, in word, in conversation, in charity, in spirit, in faith, in purity. Till I come, give attendance to reading, to exhortation, to doctrine. Neglect not the gift that is in thee, which was given thee by prophecy, with the laying on of the hands of the presbytery. Meditate upon these things; give thyself wholly to them; that thy profiting may appear to all.*

1 Tim 6:11-12 *But thou, O man of God, flee these things; and follow after righteousness, godliness, faith, love, patience, meekness. Fight the good fight of faith, lay hold on eternal life, whereunto thou art also called, and*

hast professed a good profession before many witnesses.

Here we see that we don't automatically have godliness, love, and patience. He wants us to follow after Him and not go before Him. He wants us to flee from the things that are not of God. Flee means to run.

2 Tim. 2:10 *Therefore I endure all things for the elect's sakes, that they may also obtain the salvation which is in Christ Jesus with eternal glory.*

When Paul talks about enduring all things for the elects sake he is not talking about sickness. What would sickness accomplish in the lives of the elect? What does Paul mean by all this? When we endure things, to me that means there is an end to it. The usual outcome of cancers and many sicknesses leads to death. This is not the kind of endurance Paul refers to. Paul is referring to the harsh words of people and the persecution of those around him. This is not always easy to do.

Heb 4:14 *Seeing then that we have a great high priest, that is passed into the heavens, Jesus the Son of God, let us hold fast our profession.*

Heb 6:1-3 *Therefore leaving the principles of the doctrine of Christ, let us go on unto perfection; not laying again the foundation of repentance from dead works, and of faith toward God, Of the doctrine of baptisms, and of laying on of hands, and of resurrection of the dead, and of eternal judgment. And this will we do, if God permit.*

Jude 20-21 *20 But ye, beloved, building up yourselves on your most holy faith, praying in the Holy Ghost, 21 Keep yourselves in the love of God, looking for the mercy of our Lord Jesus Christ unto eternal life.*

How is it that we receive His mercy? Not by being on our face for days in guilty confessions, but by holding fast to that profession of His faith, the faith of Jesus Christ, and building ourselves up in it. It is His faith we now have. We don't have to muster anything up, get more faith, and pray for more faith. We have THE FAITH of Our Lord living inside us. He gave it to us, as just another one of His free gifts for the taking. Doesn't that take a huge burden off you? As believers we are all given the faith of Jesus Christ. For years I thought I must not have enough faith. Now, after studying the word, I see it is another one of His gifts to us. Faith -- isn't that awesome? The truth sets us free.

The definition of Trial in the Strong's Concordance of the Bible is spiritual test, a mountain, a testing by implication, (acts of testing something) approved, trustiness, experience, proof. (2 Cor. 8:2)

To investigate, examine, prove, tempt, try (trial) (Eze 21:13) Through the idea of piercing, a test, i.e. - piers = attempt, experience, assaying, trial. (Heb 11:36)

The definition of Saleud in Strong's Concordance is to disturb, incite, move, shake, (together) which can (NOT) be shaken, stir up. (Job 9:23)

2 Cor 8:2 *How that in a great trial of affliction the abundance of their joy and their deep poverty abounded unto the riches of their liberality.*

If you have experienced a life threatening illness I bet you were not experiencing joy. God tells us the word of God is our instructor. When a life changing experience happens by my reading the word of God, there is joy that comes from that! Just as a child learns through the gentle guidance of the words of a father, they can experience joy. We have learned something new. It's a new revelation and understanding to us, especially when it is something really incredible. Our hearts are joyful. God does not bring conviction to us through His word, He says our own hearts do that for us. God, instructs and teaches us through His word.

Even when our trial is brought about by others who do not agree with us, and come against our precious Jesus in us, there is joy. Sickness? There is no joy in that! You could attempt to lie and say, "Oh, yes, I received so much joy from experiencing a sickness." Really? I don't think anyone could say that during the sickness. Perhaps after, when you took the opportunity to seek God and finally spent some time with Him. It's His word that brings comfort and joy.

1 Peter 1:7 *That the trial of your faith, being much more precious than of gold that perisheth, though it be tried (tested and proved to be reliable, useful or correct) with fire, might be found unto praise and honour and glory at the appearing of Jesus Christ:*

John 8:32 *And ye shall know the truth, and the truth shall make you free.*

Romans 10:17 *So then faith cometh by hearing, and hearing by the Word of God.*

God could not and will not do something He told us to do. He's given us the authority. He's given us His word to show us the truth, the truth that brings freedom, freedom from sickness and disease, freedom from the lies and deception of Satan and the world.

The definition of Tribulation: trouble (an annoying or frustrating or catastrophic event), not sickness and disease or affliction of any kind.

Matthew 13:21 *Yet hath he not root in himself, but dureth for a while: for when tribulation or persecution ariseth because of the word, by and by he is offended.*

In the last days there will once again be tribulation to a lost and dying people. They were already dead in their unbelief, but His people will not face the same tribulations. I do not want to confess to say that I know if His people will be taken out of this world when the final tribulation comes, but I do know that no matter what, whether we are here or already with God, His hand will be upon us. If we are still here, we will be strong and able to withstand anything that is coming against us and we will be a testimony to those who do not believe. In times of flooding or fires or other tribulations, we will stand, not because of anything we do, but because we have the power of God living inside each of us who believe. I can command the floods and fires to leave me and my household alone.

John 16:33 *These things I have spoken unto you, that in me ye might have peace. In the world ye shall have tribulation: but be of good cheer; I have overcome the world. Amen*

2 Corinthians 1:4 *Who comforteth us in all our tribulation, that we may be able to comfort them which are in any trouble, by the comfort wherewith we ourselves are comforted of God.*

Romans 12:12 *Rejoicing in hope; patient in tribulation; continuing instant in prayer;*

The Old Covenant brought death to a sinful people; the New Covenant is one of love, grace, faith and life.

Rom 8:28 (NIV) *And we know that in all things God works for the good of those who love him, who have been called according to his purpose.*

This scripture has been misused to represent our Lord bringing sickness on His people to teach them that it will be for God's glory as you endure or even die from sickness and disease. I am not saying that we may not suffer persecution at the hand of people but it is not to my God's glory that I should say He is the one who killed a young mother in a car accident, or struck her with cancer or let a child die from Leukemia. He is not the author of such things. Be convinced! He is the author of blessings and Satan is the author of sickness and disease. Remember, we have authority over all of the things Satan may try to bring against us.

Ephesians 6:11 *Put on the whole armor of God, that ye may be able to stand against the wiles of the devil.*

The definition of wiles is: a trick, artifice, or stratagem meant to fool, trap, or entice; device, artful or beguiling behavior, deceitful cunning; trickery. The only thing Satan has is wiles. Deceit and lies through his cunning, enticing lies.

We are now under that New Covenant, a covenant of grace. His grace and mercies are new every day. If I have sounded redundant at times, it is only because I want this to become such a part of you. I want the things of God to be solidified in your heart and head.

Hebrews 4:16 *Let us therefore come boldly unto the throne of grace, that we may obtain mercy, and find grace to help in time of need.*

Mercy = a disposition to be kind and forgiving; motivates compassion, something for which to be thankful - alleviation of distress.

Grace = kindness and compassion; free and unmerited favor.

Lamentations 3: 21-25 *This I recall to my mind, therefore have I hope. It is of the Lord's mercies that we are not consumed, because His compassions fail not. They are new every morning: great is thy faithfulness. The Lord is my portion, saith my soul; therefore will I hope in Him. The Lord is good unto them that wait for Him, to the soul that seeketh Him.*

Hebrews 10:17 *And their sins and iniquities will I remember no more.*

He is no longer holding our sins against us. He's forgotten all about them, for all of us, for all time. The sins that I committed yesterday, today, and the ones I'll commit tomorrow and next week.

I most likely will commit some kind of sin. I love Him so very much and try to live a life worthy of being called His, but I am still in the flesh and our God knows this, and that is why He finally had to send His Son to take care of all the sins of the world. He sent His word (His Son) not a trial, testing, or tribulation, not a sickness or disease.

John 3:17 *For God sent not his Son into the world to condemn the world; but that the world through him might be saved.* (Saved = Sozo = healed, prosperous, forgiven and set free).

I agree that when we face trials in our lives, we can turn to God for help. Often it takes sickness or disease or something traumatic in many people's lives for them to begin looking to God for help. Often it is our last hope for life. This is entirely different. It is not God giving us these things to train us or teach us, but in our own desperation or trauma we turn to Him, finally, for help, this is when we see many people give their lives to Him. We then hear people say, "See how God used that to get her/him to turn to Him." Or "Look how God used that to teach him/her." God did not do that. You finally got it through your brain that He is the only way, the only answer for all that is wrong in this world and in your life. Out of your own muck you reached out to Him and He said, "finally." Healed, prospered, forgave, and set you free. That is if you will take all He has! It's okay that it takes some of us to turn to Him out of desperation. However you do it, it's awesome. He is the only answer we ever need. He is all the healing we will ever need, not a doctor, lawyer, or Indian chief. He is everything and has everything for us.

1 John 2:2 *And he is the propitiation for our sins: and not for ours only, but also for the sins of the whole world.*

If God was causing the sicknesses, then don't you think that everyone who suffers tragedy, sickness, or the death of a loved one would be serving God. But since it is not God bringing these things on, this is why you do not see all turning to Him in these times.

Many believers only take a little from Him and do not want to go on to the great things. I find this sad. They are not going to hell, they still have a life in heaven with God, they will just get to heaven faster. They will not partake in the incredible awesome life He has for us right here, right now. Many don't know that His life is attainable for us now. They still think it is for the here-after.

Don't get in my way as I go on to the greater and as I get to live in the health, prosperity, freedoms, and forgiveness that He has put before me everyday as I choose to walk in His wonderful marvelous ways. If the way you have been doing things and believing is not getting the same results I am seeing or that Andrew Wommack, Smith Wigglesworth, John G. Lake and Mike Millers are seeing, perhaps you should look to Jesus and take heed to what I have been sharing. You will be so blessed by what He has for you. Your children and their children will be blessed.

1 Peter 2:24 *Who his own self bare our sins in his own body on the tree, that we, being dead to sins, should live unto righteousness: by whose stripes ye were healed.*

1 John 4:10 *Herein is love, not that we loved God, but that He loved us, and sent his Son to be the propitiation for our sins.*

1 Cor 15:1-2 *Brothers, I want to remind you of the gospel... because the gospel will save you only if you keep believing exactly what I preached to you--believing anything else will not lead to anything.*

The Gospel is the almost too good to be true good news of Jesus Christ. He is no longer holding our sins against us; we are new creatures in Christ, healed, and prosperous, forgiven and set free.

1 John 5:18 *We know that anyone born of God does not continue to sin; the one who was born of God keeps him safe, and the evil one does not touch him.*

We all sin except the Son of God, so what was He talking about here? He was letting us know that our sins are no longer held against us. We are not stricken with sickness by the hand of God because we sin. Yes sin can bring us to a place of receiving sickness in our body. Bitterness can cause the cells in our body to respond to sickness. Repenting, turning away from that, and looking again to our Lord can open us up to now receive His gift of healing.

THE CONVENANT OF GRACE is defined as:

Favor, kindness, friendship (Genesis 6:8; 18:3; 19:19; 2 Timothy 1:9).

The gospel as distinguished from the law (John 1:17; Romans 6:14; 1 Peter 5:12).

God's forgiving mercy (Romans 11:6; Ephesians 2:5).

Gifts freely bestowed by God; as miracles, prophecy, tongues (Romans 15:15; 1 Corinthians 15:10; Ephesians 3:8).

A glorious reward in the worship of Christ when his work was done (Philippians 2:6-11)

His goodness toward those who have no claim on, nor reason to expect, divine favor.

Grace is derived from the Greek charis. The New Testament writers used charis pre-eminently of that kindness by which God bestows favors even upon the ill-deserving, and grants to sinners the pardon of their offences, and bids them to accept eternal salvation through Christ.

2 Peter 1:2 *Grace and peace be multiplied unto you through the knowledge of God, and of Jesus our Lord.*

There are still those who are perverting the grace of God, denying His existence and most of all the work He accomplished at the cross for us - who believe.

Persecution is another thing altogether. Jesus suffered 'persecution' because of His stand for the Father and for this, we too, will be persecuted.

Matthew 13:21 *Yet hath he not root in himself, but dureth for a while: for when tribulation or persecution ariseth because of the word, by and by he is offended.*

Mark 4:17 *And have no root in themselves, and so endure but for a time: afterward, when affliction or persecution ariseth for the word's sake, immediately they are offended.*

I have given you lots of scripture to show that God is a good God; He does not put sickness or disease upon any of His people. I hope that you are convinced. This is a key to receiving your healing and freedom. If you still think that God is the one who allows all these things to come upon you and that the sovereignty of God is what keeps people from being healed, you will most likely not receive these things for yourself. God is sovereign, in that He is the greatest God, the great I Am and all that we have, we have because of Him. If you think sovereign means He is in total control of everything in this world, you are mistaken; this will keep you from receiving. He has given us the power and authority, His power and authority, yet He needs us to appropriate that power to heal the sick and, raise the dead. When your understanding of God's sovereignty is clear, you will have healing and you will do the greater.

Prayer: "Thank you God for sending your Son, that I have life and life more abundantly. Thank you for your incredible gifts to us who believe. Thank you that I am bold and I walk in your kind of love always. I want to know you more and to know your truths."
Amen.

Additional Scripture references.

2 Cor. 5:19 *To wit, that God was in Christ, reconciling the world unto himself, not imputing their trespasses unto them; and hath committed unto us the word of reconciliation.*

James 5:13-*15 Is any among you afflicted? let him pray. Is any merry? let him sing psalms. Is any sick among you? let him call for the elders of the church; and let them pray over him, anointing him with oil in the name of the Lord: And the prayer of faith shall save the sick, and the Lord shall raise him up; and if he have committed sins, they shall be forgiven him. Amen*

Hebrews 11:36 *And others had trial of cruel mockings and scourgings, yea, moreover of bonds and imprisonment:*

Colossians 3:24 *Knowing that of the Lord ye shall receive the reward of the inheritance: for ye serve the Lord Christ.*

Hebrews 1:4 *Being made so much better than the angels, as he hath by inheritance obtained a more excellent name than they.*

Hebrews 10:23 *Let us hold fast the profession of our faith without wavering; (for he is faithful that promised)*

Romans 2:9 *Tribulation and anguish, upon every soul of man that doeth evil, of the Jew first, and also of the Gentile*

Matthew 13:21 *Yet hath he not root in himself, but dureth for a while: for when tribulation or persecution ariseth because of the word, by and by he is offended.*

Matthew 24:21 *For then shall be great tribulation, such as was not since the beginning of the world to this time, no, nor ever shall be.*

Romans 5:3 *And not only so, but we glory in tribulations also: knowing that tribulation worketh patience;*

2 Peter 3:18 *But grow in grace, and in the knowledge of our Lord and Saviour Jesus Christ. To him be glory both now and for ever. Amen.*

Jude 1:4 *For there are certain men crept in unawares, who were before of old ordained to this condemnation, ungodly men, turning the grace of our God into lasciviousness, and denying the only Lord God, and our Lord Jesus Christ.*

2 Corinthians 12:10 *Therefore I take pleasure in infirmities, in reproaches, in necessities, in persecutions, in distresses for Christ's sake: for when I am weak, then am I strong.*

Matthew 6:33 *But first seek the kingdom/rule of God, and his righteousness; and all these things shall be added unto you.*

2 Corinthians 8:2 *Moreover, brethren, we do you to wit of the grace of God bestowed on the churches of Macedonia; How that in a great trial of affliction the abundance of their joy and their deep poverty abounded unto the riches of their liberality. For to their power, I bear record, yea, and beyond their power they were willing of themselves; Praying us with much intreaty that we would receive the gift, and take upon us the fellowship of the ministering to the saints.*

Deuteronomy 4:30 *When thou art in tribulation, and all these things are come upon thee, even in the latter days, if thou turn to the Lord thy God, and shalt be obedient unto his voice;*

2 Corinthians 7:4 *Great is my boldness of speech toward you, great is my glorying of you: I am filled with comfort, I am exceeding joyful in all our tribulation.*

Note: In Romans 2:9 "tribulation and anguish" are the penal sufferings that shall overtake the wicked. In Matthew 24:21, 29, the word denotes the calamities that were to attend the destruction of Jerusalem.

Chapter 9

Prayer

As I was spending time with God tonight, I thought about all the times I hear myself and others praying in a way that is wrong. God has given us the authority and power and we are still begging and asking Him to do things that He has told us to do. I have been accused may times in the past of "always praying about 'e v e r y t h i n g!' It has been a big part of my life since I came to know our LORD. I will pray over everything. It is my conversation with our Lord -- it is my way of conversing with Him about everything. He says in, 1 Thessalonians 5:17 Pray without ceasing. I am often even made fun of because I will just stop and Pray when someone even mentions a need, a want, a hurt. What does God say about praying, how to pray, when to pray. Am I wrong in what I do? Am I following God's Word in Prayer? What does He say?

My prayer life began to change as God was teaching me in His Word how it is that He wants us to pray and what it is that He has already done for us. My prayers are usually to thank Him for His finished work now instead of pleading with Him for a need. He doesn't want us begging Him for things -- He told us to speak to the mountains. I had someone ask me, "What do you mean by mountains?" I explained that God says the mountains are anything in which we want to see move or change, such as a sickness, a pain or finances. When we pray for them to move, it may sound something like, "Thank you God that You have already provided all the healing I will ever need or have. I command this pain to leave in the Name of Jesus Christ. Amen."

An acquaintance recently said she was going to start praying the same way that she heard me pray; however I saw one difference. I was thanking Him, believing that He had already done it. She was thanking

Him hoping that He would answer the prayer. Hope in the Lord is a confident expectation. The world's hope that I had learned about was 'wishful thinking' at best.

Jesus didn't pray for those who were sick. He healed them! There is a big difference in just praying a prayer, such as, "God please heal this person," and speaking to the illness and commanding it to leave. He never told us to ask Him to heal, He told us to go and heal the sick and raise the dead. Jesus didn't ask the Father in Heaven, He told sickness to go, He commanded healing to come.

If I continue to pray for something He has already done for me, I am saying to our God in Heaven, "I don't believe you have done this, so I am going to have to keep praying for this until I see you do it." It seems I am actually calling Him a liar when I pray this way. That is a prayer of unbelief.

Once you get a revelation of what Jesus has already done for you and has already provided for you at the cross, it changes your prayer life. We no longer beg God in our prayers to do the things He already provided for us. You can begin to thank Him, praise Him, and rest in that finished work.

Here is where the law of 'seed, time, and harvest,' comes in for us. When we pray and thank Him for something, or we speak directly to something and take our authority over it to change, we have 'planted the seed.' Now there is a time before the harvest. Time is God's appointed blessing for us to believe. It may be only a matter of seconds if we believe, or it may be a few weeks if we have something that may be hindering our belief system. His 'time' allows us to believe. We may have some unbelief that will hinder the manifestation of His provision. It is already ours, but we may not feel healed. The time allows us to believe, even without feeling. It was there all along. We needed to know that and the time allows us to come to this understanding.

What are His instructions for me on how to pray?

Matthew 6:7-15 *But when ye pray, use not vain repetitions, as the heathen do: for they think that they shall be heard for their much speaking. Be not ye therefore like unto them: for your Father knoweth what things ye have need of, before ye ask him. After this manner therefore pray ye: Our Father which art in heaven, Hallowed be thy name. Thy kingdom come. Thy will be done in earth, as it is in heaven. Give us this day our daily bread. And forgive us our debts, as we forgive our debtors. And lead us not into temptation, but deliver us from evil: For thine is the kingdom, and the power, and the glory, for ever. Amen. For if ye forgive men their trespasses, your heavenly Father will also forgive you: But if ye forgive not men their trespasses, neither will your Father forgive your trespasses.*

1 Thessalonians 3:10 *Night and day praying exceedingly that we might see your face, and might perfect that which is lacking in your faith?*

He tells us not to use repetition as we pray. I know some religious people will take offense to this as well, for they continue to pray the same things over and over. Repetition is not going to hurt them, but it's certainly not how God asks us to pray, and I see no benefit in it.

I have been told it is offensive to others when I pray out loud thanking God for what He has already done. They feel like I am judging the way they are. This is so far from what I feel or believe. I was simply taking the power and authority given to us as believers and if you are not going to take it, I will try to help you take and receive what you are in need of. We are such sensitive people. Many are offended too easily. The offense may be that they truly do not believe that God has already provided all the healing and provision for them and their unbelief is convicting them.

I find that people want me to wail and travail over their affliction and when I don't, they find this offensive as well. I will have compassion for their misery but I will not allow the Enemy to take a foothold in their lives if I can help it. I desire that no one should be offended by what God has already provided and take offense at how I pray believing that it's already a done deal! So forgive me if I offend you, but I would rather offend you than let you die in your affliction. (Even Jesus offended.)

Philippians 1:4 *Always in every prayer of mine for you all making request with joy,*

Here we see that when we make a request through prayer, that it is with joy. Joy connotes a happy ending -- not the travailing and moaning I have often heard in 'intercessory prayer meetings.' I am not against intercessory prayer, I just think it has been done wrong. There is no scriptural reference for what I see going on at these meetings. I haven't seen the same results come from these type of prayers as I have since I began to thank Him and praise Him for what He has done. I started believing in His finished work and thanking Him for it and took the authority and used His power over my situations. When I spoke to my hand and wrist to be healed is a good example of this. I am not commanding God to do something. I am taking the authority and power He has already provided for me and agreeing with Him.

In the New Testament God says Jesus is our only mediator now.

1 Timothy 2:5 *"For there is one God, and one mediator between God and men, the man Christ Jesus."*

I have the best mediator / intercessor. His Name is Jesus. People are often begging God to turn his wrath from them, a country, or America because we are such a sinful people and nation. Yes we are sinful, but sin is no longer a factor for us or for God. Sin has been taken care of through the atonement of Jesus Christ. We are no longer stoned to death because of our sins. We are only held accountable for what we believe. "Wow," you may say, "That's crazy."

You have just given people the go ahead to sin all they want. It is just the opposite really. Once you recognize the incredible gift of a loving God who took care of all your sins through the sacrifice of His Son, this love inspires us not to sin. Not that we won't ever sin again, because we do! My heart's desire is not to sin because of His incredible gift of love. God is no longer mad at us, we no longer have to pray, begging Him to spare the wrath. None of us deserve this incredible gift, but there it was hanging on the cross waiting for us to take it.

People pray for family members to be saved, begging God to save them. However, He say's it's the truth that sets people free. If they don't know Him and the truth, begging God to save them is not going to work. They need to hear the Gospel, the truth for themselves. I could pray for God to send people into their path that would share the Gospel with them. But if I am able, I need to be the one to share God's truth with them. We are often fearful of rejection, or being offensive to them. I was reminded after speaking at a meeting, that 'even Jesus offended people.' I took it as a compliment, because I had offended two particular people at this meeting, but my flesh was not happy. I don't like to offend people or make them uncomfortable but I will not compromise the word of God to do that. Again, I would rather offend in the Name of Jesus than comfort you to death!

In Corinthians we see it is not through prayer that people are saved but through preaching, preaching is not a confrontation but a gentle teaching of the truth. Preaching is not standing on a pulpit screaming at people. Preaching is sharing the truth with them of this incredible

God of the New Testament. There will be people who do not want to hear, and will take offense.

1 Corinthians 1:21 *For seeing that in the wisdom of God the world through its wisdom knew not God, it was God's good pleasure through the foolishness of the preaching to save them that believe.*

Praying always puts me in relationship with God, and I am conversing with Him all day long. How wonderful that we get to do that. We get to talk to him all day. I am never lonely or bored. We always have Him to talk to and if we stop and listen, we can hear Him talk back. These conversations are wonderful. How amazing that we all get to have conversations with Him! Practice listening to His voice. Get to know Him intimately.

The past few mornings as I was talking with our Lord, He impressed upon me that praying (or speaking to the mountain) for a sickness to be healed was similar to alcoholism. What's that got to do with prayer? "When an alcoholic first starts drinking, it is much easier for them to seek the Father and be delivered from this than it is when they begin to entertain it and to think on it, which then often leads to doing it. When we first have a sickness or a disease tries to come upon us, it is easier to come against it in the very beginning, than when we contemplate on it, think about it and nurse it. (The battle begins in the mind.) It takes more to come against it. Later as I was talking with our Lord again, He impressed upon me that I often have felt things early in a sickness, or an attack of some kind. I have always been very aware of my body. Because I did not know God's truth's on this, I entertained it, thought about it and it became worse. It is nice that I feel things early, I can then come against them right away. What I used to think was a bad thing in my life has now become something good. I will pray by taking authority over this sickness, pain or infirmity right away, commanding it to leave -- I am no longer asking or begging God to remove these things from me.

God wants us to seek Him, rebuke the sickness, command it to go, speak to the mountain. Then, thank and praise Him for all He has done, for the finished work at the cross -- don't think about the pain, the sickness or what ever may be trying to come upon you -- instead think about and seek the Father's face. Meditate on what God says about healing. When we entertained sickness and sinful things, they can take a foothold in our lives, just as an alcoholic becomes worse, when he entertains his demon. As we are learning God's ways, we want the Father to quicken and show us when these attacks and the lies from Satan come in from the very beginning, so we can counter them with the truth of what our God says and the truth of what our Jesus did.

We have often misunderstood the concept of "intercessory prayer." God says He is our intercessor. I will seek Him and not someone to pray for this or that. Though please don't misunderstand, I still believe in prayer, however, I no longer ask many to pray for me because of what God has been teaching me. Because I feel many of the prayers people pray are 'worthless and empty,' clanging symbols, filled with unbelief. I hear people going on and on in prayer, I see myself and others tuning them out. Once the anointing or blessing has left and we start praying in our flesh I find it boring, unnecessary and worthless. Ahhh!!! Even as I write this, I know I will offend those who have often come to me and said they are 'intercessors' and then go on and on and on in prayer! I think some people do that to appease or 'please' the flesh in themselves and others. To convince them or you about our awesome God, be convinced yourself! I know I keep telling you that. I want you to get it! I want you to be completely convinced!

When I am praying for someone, if I simply command a sickness to leave or speak to a pain in a person's body and stop there, will they be disappointed?

Ramblings are worthless. I would much rather stand and speak truth in 2 seconds than ramble on with empty nothing words for ten minutes to please someone's flesh. I guess some may be offended, but I don't speak harshly over them. I am always in His presence and try to always speak with grace and love, though it wasn't always that way. I do share the truth to them if they need to hear that first so that they may believe. I would much rather have a five second prayer, prayed in faith and belief, in the power and authority of our incredible Lord, than the unbelieving ramblings of someone who calls themself an intercessor, who is trying to convince themselves and you that God might do something here through their ramblings.

I have been in prayer groups calling themselves intercessors. I saw no fruit. What I did see were men begging God to come and move the mountains, to heal the sick, to cast out the demons. So when we do not see these things happening, another intercessory prayer meeting is called. God tells us to heal the sick, speak to the mountains, and cast out demons. He tells us the truth is what sets people free. Go share the truth, thanking Him and praising Him for the finished work of His Son. Take the authority and power He's given us and command sickness to leave. This is prayer.

Command the mountain to go, tell the demons to flee, raise the dead, heal the sick, open blind eyes. He spoke truth in love, which frees us. He laid hands on the sick and healed them. He spoke a word -- and they were healed. Except in the towns where there was much unbelief, Jesus could do no mighty works there, because of their unbelief.

Prayer is not the same as what I had been taught to believe as a child. It is not me coming to God with all my wants and desires and asking Him to do something about them. It is not begging and pleading with God to raise the dead, heal the sick and bring revival. But what is it you may ask? If God says to pray without ceasing, and to pray for all things at all times, what will I pray and how will it look? He tells us to go heal the sick, He doesn't say to pray and ask Him to do it. We are not to petition God to perform some miracle -- it is always God doing things through us. The reason He sent His Son, the reason He had to come as a man is because He made a covenant with man that He now gave man the authority and power. It is His power living inside of me.

Prayer is simply thanking God for the finished work of Jesus Christ on the cross, agreeing and believing in what he did. Prayer could be in song or worship. Thank You God that we are healed, prospered, forgiven and set free! How incredibly marvelous and simple it is. We no longer have to be lying prostrate in prayer for two hours, for God to answer us. He has already answered us, it is finished. We just thank Him and believe. I love Him so much that all day is prayer to me. I consider it all joy to be spending every day with my best friend, my Savior and Daddy, thanking Him for his grace and love.

We can ask God to send laborers into the life of a friend or someone to share the Gospel, the almost too good to be true news of Jesus Christ with them. But if God tells us to do it, we should not ask Him to send someone else. My heart's desire is that you understand and receive all that you have as a believer in Jesus Christ. If you are not a believer yet, I pray that you would look to Jesus and ask Him into your life, into your heart, and believe in His finished work that He provided for you at the cross. He gave His life for you and me. It's a wonderful life.

I remember as a new believer, I heard someone say they are up at 5:00 a.m. and go to their prayer closet and begin to pray. I never really asked them what it was or how it was they prayed. I just remember thinking I could never do that, and that maybe I will never get to receive from God because I wasn't a 'prayer warrior' like they were. But I see what a lie from Satan that is. I often do get up at 4:00 a.m. and I will just read God's word, spend time with Him and listen to Him. Sometimes I ask for Him to send people into the lives of those I can't be with to share the truth with them in a way they will receive and understand it.

Ephesians 1:17-19.

I love to do word studies as this helps me understand what God really means in His word and then I spend time thanking Him. Prayer, praise and thanksgiving are my positive response to what God has already done.

Mark 16:15 *And he said unto them, Go ye into all the world, and preach the gospel to every creature.*

Prayer: "Thank You, God! I love you."

Scripture references

Hebrews 8:6 *But now hath he obtained a more excellent ministry, by how much also he is the mediator of a better covenant, which was established upon better promises.*

1 Thessalonians 1:2 *We give thanks to God always for you all, making mention of you in our prayers;*

Philemon 1:4 *I thank my God, making mention of thee always in my prayers,*

Romans 8:26 *Likewise the Spirit also helpeth our infirmities: for we know not what we should pray for as we ought: but the Spirit itself maketh intercession for us with groanings which cannot be uttered.*

Ephesians 1:16 *Cease not to give thanks for you, making mention of you in my prayers;*

Philippians 1:4 *Always in every prayer of mine for you all making request with joy,*

Philippians 4:6 *Be careful for nothing; but in every thing by prayer and supplication with thanksgiving let your requests be made known unto God.*

Acts 16:25 *And at midnight Paul and Silas prayed, and sang praises unto God: and the prisoners heard them.*

Luke 20:47 *Which devour widows' houses, and for a shew make long prayers: the same shall receive greater damnation.*

Psalm 100:4 *Enter into his gates with thanksgiving, and into his courts with praise: be thankful unto him, and bless his name.*

2 Corinthians 1:11 *Ye also helping together by prayer for us, that for the gift bestowed upon us by the means of many persons thanks may be given by many on our behalf.*

Ephesians 6:18 *Praying always with all prayer and supplication in the Spirit, and watching thereunto with all perseverance and supplication for all saints;*

Philippians 1:4 *Always in every prayer of mine for you all making request with joy,...*

Hebrews 9:15 *And for this cause he is the mediator of the new testament, that by means of death, for the redemption of the transgressions that were under the first testament, they which are called might receive the promise of eternal inheritance.*

Hebrews 12:24 *And to Jesus the mediator of the new covenant, and to the blood of sprinkling, that speaketh better things than that of Abel.*

Chapter 10

How to Keep That Which Has Already Been Provided By Jesus

Have you often wondered why it is that many people lose their healing once God has delivered them? The manifestation has taken place and they are set free, living in peace, joy and health. It makes me sad and even a bit angry to see people healed and then years, months, or even weeks later die or have the sickness return, and they lose their peace and freedom. I will be focusing on mainly physical healing in this chapter, but this applies to all areas of our lives, as peace, emotional healing, joy, health, love, bitterness and prosperity.

With my own healing I remember as soon as I was healed, the skeptics made sure that I was aware of the consequences of not having chemotherapy or radiation, and what the next stage of this cancer might mean for me. I just kept saying "no," in my spirit and spoke encouragement and truth to my mind and body. I continued to repeat to myself the truth of God's word and the scriptures I had remembered, I did not let the lies and the fear take root to steal my healing. I never once thought that God allowed this to teach me some lesson or what it was that I needed to learn. I looked to His truths and His words.

My own family members, friends and well meaning loved ones thought that I should be doing some sort of follow-up medical treatment. The doctor's diagnoses was cancer, but they soon forgot that I was 'healed' completely and miraculously by the Lord, and once He heals you, it is finished. I was convinced! It was finished at the cross! I personally didn't need to have any follow-ups done.

Jesus was my doctor, my healer, chemo, and provider in every way. He provided everything at the cross.

3 John 2 *Beloved, I wish above all things that thou mayest prosper and be in good health, even as my soul prospers.*

Does this mean that I didn't have doubt at times or that the enemy didn't 'try' to bring things back upon me? He did try and he continues at times to try to lie and deceive me into believing his junk. I continue to stand on the healing that is mine. I continue to look at what God says in His word and not what friends, family and others have to say. I will listen when it is truth spoken to me. Their truth may be different than God's. I guard my heart with all diligence.

Proverbs 4:23 *Keep thy heart with all diligence; for out of it are the issues of life.*

God has taken me to the story of the blind man in Behtsaida many times. Jesus took the blind man out of the city. He prefaced this by saying "this town was one of two that had more un-belief in them than any others."

(Luke 10:13) (Mark 8:23)

Jesus could have healed the man anywhere, unless of course it takes something on our part. Jesus led the man out of Behtsaida and then prays for him. He then asks him, "What do you see?" The man replies, "I see men walking as trees" (his healing was not complete yet). Jesus then prays for him the second time, laying his hands on his eyes and asks him again what he saw. The man saw clearly. Now his healing was complete. Jesus then tells the man not to return to Bethsaida. Why? Remember how He had to take him out to be healed, and had prefaced these passages with letting us know that this town was filled with unbelief. I recognize that town in believers and many of the churches today. Many receive their healing, but when a negative word is spoken or people who doubt God's Word and truth come along side of them they begin to ask "Were you really healed? Don't you think you should return to a doctor?" I believe the blind man would have lost his healing had he returned to the town of Bethsaida. Jesus did not want that to happen to him. I believe time spent away from the unbelief and sitting under the truth of Jesus and His teaching would build him up and he would have been strong enough in his belief to return. It was to his benefit to not return at this time.

When I was believing for my healing, I needed to pull away from those who walked in unbelief. I needed to set my focus on Jesus and His truths. I had to turn off the TV, shut out the noise of the world and those around me as much as I possibly could. I needed to feed my belief, and starve my unbelief. Well meaning friends said things that made me cringe with unbelief at times, and I needed to get back in the word to overcome the lies. I remember one friend say "don't you think you now have the same thing your father died from?" This was unbelief, lies and fear trying to speak into my life. I am pretty sure the now seeing man from Bethsaida would have heard many of the same things from well meaning friends and family. They may have said "We are only trying to help you." I think people's hearts want the best for us; they just don't know God's truths yet. Most of the church still looks at life through their five senses. If they can't hear, taste, smell, see or feel it, they don't believe it is so.

If I had listened to all the lies that the enemy came against me with I could have lost my healing. Instead of thinking on the possibilities my friends, family and the medical community gave me, I chose to think on all God says I have. Why do we see many who have once been healed lose their healing? The Enemy comes to steal, kill and destroy, and he will use well meaning friends and others to do it. He cannot do anything without a willing body to work through. Some of those who are being used by Satan to steal your healing do not even recognize that is what they are doing.

Philippians 4:8 *Finally, brethren, whatsoever things are true, whatsoever things are honest, whatsoever things are just, whatsoever things are pure, whatsoever things are lovely, whatsoever things are of good report; if there be any virtue, and if there be any praise, think on these things.*

I chose to look to God and what He says. I wasn't seeing anything lovely about cancer treatment. I have heard more people die from chemotherapy and radiation than of the actual cancer. I don't know if this is true or not.

In Daniel 9 we see that the first time Daniel prayed for something it happened in 3 minutes the second time it took 3 weeks. There was a time for him to believe for that healing to manifest, a time to overcome some unbelief. When I prayed for my husband it took two weeks, but actually it was a year from the time he was diagnosed for him to come to the truth of 'God's healing' and then to ask for it. Thankfully it was before he died. Amen! When I prayed for my hip it took three months for the manifestation to come. I do not know all the things I was entertaining in my thoughts only that there was some unbelief that had entered in through some words spoken to me by a friend. There may be many factors that keep us from receiving healing or prosperity when we first pray and speak to the problem. Don't allow yourself or others to abort the miracle before its time. Keep standing! Here is where the time is working for you. The law of seed, time and harvest. Plant the truth in you and water it with the truth as much as possible.

How do we keep our healing, and the health that Jesus has already provided?

What is it that you want to believe in? Do you put your belief and trust in doctors, psychotherapist, medicine, vitamins, or in Jesus Christ and His healing power? Be convinced through the Word that as a believer you have been given all the healing power and authority of Jesus and it is living inside of you. It's not just a chosen few that have these gifts. Every one of us has them and as believers we can appropriate them if we believe.

Most of us would say that we want to believe in Jesus, and want to trust in His complete healing for us.

How many of us take the time and effort to focus on Him and not on the medical field? One day an unbelieving Christian had spoken a simple word of unbelief to me, it was a simple statement! I entertained the thought for a moment. For that moment fear gripped me and I began to think, "Perhaps I am stupid for trusting in God, maybe God created doctors so that I can trust and rely on them?" As soon as I thought this, I remember the Father taking my face in His hands and looking into my eyes. He spoke to me saying "Keep your focus on me Connie, and all the things of the world, the lies of the Enemy, sickness, disease, and all of that will be as nothing." The visual picture He gave me was of Him with my face in His hands looking into His face and Him looking into my eyes. The things of Satan (sickness, disease, etc.) were so tiny and far behind me, they were as nothing. I continue to picture this whenever fears or unbelief are spoken to me, or I hear a negative word about who I am in Him and my inheritance as His daughter.

I believe in nutrition and eating well: eating more of what God made and less of what man made. There was a time that I relied heavily on supplements and was spending hundreds of dollars a month on them. God wanted me to totally trust in the provision of healing He has for me. I stopped the supplements completely and relied on Jesus 100% with wisdom. I don't believe supplements are bad, and in fact actually think they are good, but my trust was now in them and not totally on God. I needed to get rid of them for a time and just focus on Him. I now take very few supplements; my health is from relying on the finished work of Jesus Christ. I try to eat healthy and would like to exercise more. I know we should take care of this 'earth' our bodies. When we do eat something unhealthy I believe God has given us a way out of its consequences (within reason). He says "you can drink deadly poison and it will not harm you."

Mark 16:18 *They shall take up serpents; and if they drink any deadly thing, it shall not hurt them; they shall lay hands on the sick, and they shall recover.*

Now I don't believe we should test this and go drink poison, that's just ignorance, but if you should drink some poison on accident, you have God's word to stand on. I have well meaning people say to me when they do not see the healing right away, that Jesus chose Luke the physician as a disciple so we must need doctors. I am not against doctors, they are for unbelievers.

Let's look at Luke. Luke was not Jewish; he was Greek by birth, well educated in the Greek culture. A medical practitioner by profession and a traveling companion of Paul and his friends. He stayed with Paul throughout Paul's second missionary trip until the time of imprisonment at Rome. He was a reliable friend of Paul, as many friends deserted Paul because of his imprisonment for the sake of the Gospel.

Luke's life is rather obscure, being a medical doctor. A man of science, he reported the medical terms of illnesses that people who were miraculously healed by Jesus had. Luke was asked to validate the story of the life of Jesus and what followed after his death. Luke also had a personal interest for he was a Christian; he was interested physically, and spiritually. Luke gave a more orderly account of different healings of people than any of the other books. He investigated each report, and heard testimonies from eyewitnesses; he chronicles accounts of God's work that he witnessed himself, and the sermons of the early preachers he had heard.

As a New Testament writer Luke is the only one who tells us the continuation of the disciple's lives after the death of Christ, and how preachers and teachers went abroad following the command of Christ. I see no account of him reporting on healings with the use of medical doctors or his own medical practices. He saw and understood the scale of God's love and of His mercy. He records more parables and events in Jesus' life than the other gospels, and many of Christ's teachings. He was detailed in his recording history, with an emphasis on dates and facts.

Although being a trained physician, and a well educated man, he was a humble and faithful person.

Luke used a medical vocabulary instinctively. In the account where the boy is said to be "thrown down" by his affliction, the Greek word Luke uses was the current medical term for convulsions. In the incident where the distraught father cries to Jesus, "Look upon my son!" the word Luke uses for "look upon" is the current medical term used of a physician seeing a patient. Like most physicians Luke was defensive of the medical profession. When the menorrhagic woman (woman with the issue of blood) approaches Jesus, Matthew and Mark tell us she had exhausted all her savings on physicians but was no better. Dr. Luke tells us the same story, but chooses to omit the part about costly medical treatment that had proved unsuccessful.

Luke shows his diagnostic work here by distinguishing between Jesus healing those who had diseases and those who were afflicted by demons. He knew whether a condition was spiritual or physical. He knew how to apply God's power to body, soul or both as needed. For Peter's mother-in-law it appears there is a hint of some sort of spiritual attack, because this is the only occasion when Jesus speaks to a disease, rebuking the fever it says in verse 39.

Luke 4:39 *And he stood over her, and rebuked the fever; and it left her: and immediately she arose and ministered unto them.*

Luke's gifts as a physician before becoming a follower of Jesus helped him to look at the miracles and healings of Jesus as no other disciple did. He was careful to report things clearly. We however do not see him recording anytime when medicine was used again. As detailed a writer that he was, if he was going back to being a medical doctor using the methods of his former teaching we would have heard about it. Yet we do not. We only see him recording all the healings of Jesus, the fact that he could see the root of the sickness is attributed to his past career. God used His talents in a new way.

What do you believe about yourself?

Do you believe Satan's lies about you? Do you believe you are cursed? Do you believe because a relative suffered from a particular disease that you to will face those same things? Remember God saying in Deuteronomy that He was taking all the cursings and leaving us His blessings. When we are born again, we are new creatures in Christ, old things are passed away, and all things become new." We no longer have to worry about the cursings or generational curses, unless we personally believe them which gives them power in our life. Because of a lack of understanding or knowledge we often believe Satan's lies, his wiles. We can follow in the footsteps of our ancestors or family, only because that is what we are taught to believe. If you are not a believer in Jesus Christ you may be facing the same things that some of your relatives did. If you are a believer in all the Jesus Christ did you now have the Holy Spirit and Jesus living inside of you, you have His power and authority, you are healed, prosperous, forgiven and set free. Believe in those things. Let the truth of who He says you are and what you have get in the way of what you have been taught and what you have believed in the past. Believe His Truths. Read the word and believe it! God's truth sets us free, not exorcisms from curses. We are already free, most do not know that.

Mark 7:13 *Making the word of God of none effect through your tradition, which ye have delivered: and many such like things do ye.*

Traditions are not all bad, but God is warning that they will make His word of no effect in our lives. You can choose to believe in all the traditions or you can choose to believe His word and His Truths.

God had already promised healing for His people in the Old Testament.

Exodus 23:25 *and ye shall serve the LORD your God, and He shall bless thy bread, and thy water; and I will take sickness away from the mist of thee.*

Psalm 105:37 *He brought them forth also with silver and gold; and there was not one feeble person among their tribes.*

Psalms 103:3 *Who forgiveth all thine iniquities; who healeth all thy diseases;*

God has forgiven all our sins and healed us, it is done! You can choose to believe that fact or what the world, and too often the church, has taught about having to deserve His healing and receiving all the benefits of His salvation. We can never be good enough or deserving of what He did. This makes us love Him even more! These are His free gifts to us. I hope that you will receive all He has for you.

Luke 9:*2 And he sent them to preach the kingdom of God, and to heal the sick.*

His Grace (walking in His blessings) is for each of us. Not just believers. It's just that as believers we have the realization of who and what we have. Or do we? God is not picking and choosing who is going to receive that healing based on how good of a person we are. It is based solely on what He did and us believing that we have nothing to do with it. God has already sent the provision for everyone on the face of the earth. The revelation that everyone has all the healing power living inside of us is a powerful tool for us to grasp. He did it all, His grace is balanced with the faith of Him living in me. God loves you, He is not mad at you. I am among the worst sinners on the face of the earth, but I finally got a true revelation of who I am, and what He did and how much He loves me. I have received my health and healing and all the benefits of this incredible loving Father. Do I always have success? Not yet, but I am expecting to.

What does God Say about our health?

3 John 1:2 *Beloved, I wish above all things that thou mayest prosper and be in health, even as thy soul prospereth.*

It is God's perfect will to have us well and prosper. God says we are already healthy, prosperous, forgiven and set free, because of who He is. That's what He desires, that's what He provided and we need to believe and receive from Him.

Luke 13:12 *And when Jesus saw her, he called her to him, and said unto her, Woman, thou art loosed from thine infirmity.*

Proverbs 16:24 *Pleasant words are as an honeycomb, sweet to the soul, and health to the bones*

Understand that we are Spirit, Soul and Body

1 Thes 5:23 *And the very God of Peace sanctify you wholly; and I pray God your whole spirit and soul and body be preserved blameless unto the coming of our Lord Jesus Christ.*

The spirit is the essence of a person; it is clothed in the body. The fact that God created us, with a spirit, a body and soul, helps us to see how God works. He is Spirit and we worship Him in spirit and in truth. We may not see it, but our spirit is the part that gets to worship and that gets to spend eternity with Him. The Holy Spirit lives in us and He shows us great and mighty things.

Romans 8:9 *But ye are not in the flesh, but in the Spirit, if so be that the Spirit of God dwell in you. Now if any man have not the Spirit of Christ, he is none of his.*

John 3:5 *Jesus answered, Verily, verily, I say unto thee, except a man be born of water and of the Spirit, he cannot enter into the kingdom of God.*

We have a body that will eventually be gone, but He still wants us to have health in this physical body to bring glory to Him. What glory is it to Him if we are sick and weak in this body? First, we are unable to go out and share the Gospel in the way He has asked us to, and second we wouldn't be a very good testimony to the incredible power of a God who said He brought salvation to the world. (Salvation = healed, prospered, forgiven, set free) Confess what you have, His healing, His prosperity, forgiveness and freedom.

Philippians 1:20 *According to my earnest expectation and my hope, that in nothing I shall be ashamed, but that with all boldness, as always, so now also Christ shall be magnified in my body, whether it be by life, or by death.*

Understand Satan's intentions

Keep resisting Satan's advances and lies. Give no

thought to his lies. Do not let him steal what God provided for you at the cross.

John 10:10 *The thief cometh not, but for to steal, and to kill, and to destroy: I am come that they might have life, and that they might have it more abundantly.*

Most of us are familiar with this scripture. Satan will try to put thoughts in your mind to doubt God. Remember this is exactly what he did to Eve in the garden. He got her to doubt God's promises and His Word to them. That's all he has! That's all he's ever had. But if Adam and Eve who met with God everyday were tempted to doubt God, how much more are we?

If your focus is on Jesus you can stop the enemy! Put your focus on the one who came to die for you in order that you might have life, and more abundantly (not on sickness and disease.) Your sorrow will turn to joy, your sickness to health, and your poverty to riches.

1 John 4:1 *Beloved, believe not every spirit, but try the spirits whether they are of God: because many false prophets are gone out into the world.*

Satan needs people! He needs a physical body, a willing vessel, whether it is a pig or a man to manifest his lies and deception through. Don't be a willing vessel for the enemy. Instead put on the whole armor so you can stand and be strong and be used by the one who loves you. We need to fill ourselves with Jesus.

Matthew 12:43-45 *When the unclean spirit is gone out of a man, he walketh through dry places, seeking rest, and findeth none. 44 Then he saith, I will return into my house from whence I came out; and when he is come, he findeth it empty, swept, and garnished. 45 Then goeth he, and taketh with himself seven other spirits more wicked than himself, and they enter in and dwell there: and the last state of that man is worse than the first. Even so shall it be also unto this wicked generation.*

Ephesians 4:27 says *"don't give place to the devil."* Jesus says to, "Take heed of what you hear and how you hear it."

Understand your situation and keep watch over your heart.

Whatever situation you may face, you have a choice. You can either turn to God and follow Him and believe what He says about you or you can follow the devil. There really are only two choices here. The devil also represents the worldly thoughts and views. Anything that does not promote the views and opinions of Jesus Christ is of Satan. It's wrong! Whatever your case is, Jesus has given us the necessary weapons to deal with it. Whether the cause is demonic, biological or a combination of both, it doesn't matter. God has healed and delivered, He has given you power and authority over it all. (Proverbs 4:20-23) When our focus is off of Jesus and we are looking at the world, it opens us up for satan's lies and deception. Satan's only power is that which we give him through his lies and deception. Jesus took care of Satan at the cross, when he descended into hell to fight the battle for us there. He won, if you haven't read the Book. We won.

Bitterness, anger and resentment can open us up to the lies of Satan. Resist hateful thoughts from the enemy. Hatred, anger and bitterness can destroy your health. When I was living in bitterness, my life was not full of God; it was focused on my own self, and the fact that someone had hurt my heart. This opened me up for the enemy. Let go of any unforgiveness, bitterness, anger and resentment. We do need to repent. But God is merciful, and provides you a way to escape punishment for your sins. God offers you the free gift of salvation. The definition of repentance means a deep sorrow, compunction, or contrition for a past sin, wrongdoing, or the like. It means to turn from the things that are not pleasing to God.

I remember trying within myself to let go and give it all to God. It wasn't working. The anger turned to resentment and then to bitterness and it grew to infest every area of my life. I was trying to do something within myself to make the anger go away. I recognize this in others now. It is sad. There is usually a cause for our anger but God wants us to give it all to Him. I simply and finally recognized I didn't know how to let go of the bitterness, so I asked God to take it one day. I said "God, I do not know how to do this! Please take this from me." It was about two weeks later when I realized the resentments and bitterness had gone from my heart. It was just gone. That simple, I asked, looked to His truths and it was gone!

Ask and it shall be given to you. Luke 11:9 And I say unto you, Ask, and it shall be given you; seek, and ye shall find; knock, and it shall be opened unto you.

The best way to have a healthy spiritual heart and to keep your healing and walk in health is to fill it with God's Word. Look at the finished work of Jesus Christ, His Grace and Faith. The action taken on our part is to simply press into what God's truths are by reading the Word and spending time with Him. Don't give up; keep on standing, standing on His truths and on His word. It is the message of His love that changes you. God's love, healing and gifts are unconditional. It does not change based on my performance. My actions do not change His love for me. When you live in sin it will open a door to Satan.

2 Cor 5:21 *For He hath made Him to be sin for us, who knew no sin; that we might be made the righteousness of God in Him.*

When we choose to believe in Christ and receive His forgiveness, it simply means we accept His punishment on our behalf. It has nothing to do with what I do. He bore our sins (took them upon himself literally) we need to accept his sacrifice and believe what He accomplished for us to receive. I kept feeding my believer, until I got it! (It = His power, authority, love, grace, mercy, joy, peace, prosperity, healing, forgiveness, and freedom.) We receive His healing, love and health the same way we received his forgiveness and salvation. God's salvation is for the ungodly, it is unconditional.

Matthew 8:17 *That it might be fulfilled which was spoken by Esaias the prophet, saying, Himself took our infirmities, an bare our sickness.*

There may be a cause for sickness to take root in our bodies, but there is also a cure through the sacrifice of Jesus Christ on the cross. There is a choice for us to make. Do we accept and choose to believe what He did for us? Start thanking Him and praising Him for what He has done! You may find I repeat myself many times, but that is only because I have had so much unbelief poured into me over the years that it has taken many repetitions of His truth in me to cancel out all the junk that was fed into me.

Learning to live in the blessings and health, and not from miracle to miracle was a process for me: I do not have all the answers, but I know who does. And I know that He wrote them down for us in His word. His Word is life and healing for all those who believe. The Bible is a revelation of His love, His heart and our inheritance.

Galatians 2:20 *I am crucified with Christ: nevertheless I live; yet not I, but Christ liveth in me: and the life which I now live in the flesh I live by The faith of the Son of God, who loved me, and gave himself for me.*

Keep yourself surrounded by belief.

1. Turn off the TV and stop reading junk!

2. Fill yourself with the Truth of God.

3. Fall in love with the Truth, with Him, and with His Word. Faith comes by hearing and hearing by the word of God.

4. Get into a spirit filled gospel preaching church. (The good news of Jesus Christ is the Gospel). Do not listen to unbelief any longer.

5. Spend more time in the Word feeding on His truths instead of studying some sickness.

6. Start praising and thanking God for His finished work.

Mark 6:1-5 *And he went out from thence, and came into his own country; and his disciples follow him. And when the Sabbath day was come, he began to teach in the synagogue: and many hearing him were astonished, saying, From whence hath this man these things? and what wisdom is this which is given unto him, that even such mighty works are wrought by his hands? Is not this the carpenter, the son of Mary, the brother of James, and Joses, and of Juda, and Simon? and are not his sisters here with us? And they were offended at him. But Jesus said unto them, a prophet is not without honour, but in his own country, and among his own kin, and in his own house. And he could there do no mighty work, save that he laid his hands upon a few sick folk, and healed them.*

How many more needed healing but because of unbelief, doubt and judgment, were unable to receive? How many followers of Jesus do not believe to receive their healing? Doubt and unbelief steals our healing, our joy and love. Whenever we see belief, we see His healings manifest. When we see unbelief we see only a few healings. Unbelief is a thief.

Keep feeding your belief.

Jesus says, to examine what you hear and how you hear what has been said.

Mark 4:24 *And he said unto them, Take heed what ye hear: with what measure ye mete, it shall be measured to you: and unto you that hear shall more be given.*

We often tend to believe everything that's spoken at the pulpit. I remember doing just that as a new believer. This was my foundation. I soon found that the more I wanted what Jesus said we were to have, the more I sought it out. I wasn't finding it where I was. I began to question what I was hearing from the pulpit, asking myself, "What else is not true?" You need to always check everything you hear with the word of God. Whether it's what I say, your pastor, or the TV evangelist. Is what you are hearing inspire faith and bring life or does it bring doubt and unbelief? Is it filled with Life or death?

If you are sitting under teaching week after week and hear that God doesn't heal today or God gives you sickness to teach you a lesson or " What sin have you not confessed?" I suggest you find a church that is sharing the true Gospel of Jesus Christ. If we had to make sure every sin we ever committed is confessed before we can be healed, or before we can receive from God and hear from Him, then not one person on the face of the earth would be healed, no one would experience salvation.

Traditions can kill you. Religion can kill you. What you don't know can kill you. God comes strongly against a powerless religion that observes just traditions and He says for us to turn away.

2 Tim 3:5 *Having a form of godliness, but denying the power thereof: from such turn away.*

Mark 7:13 *Making the word of God of none effect through your tradition, which ye have delivered: and many such like things do ye.*

7. Keep praising and thanking God for your health and all He has provided.

I continually am thanking God throughout my day. I think others find this offensive. When there is a need, praise and thank Him for the need for it has already been provided. Thank Him for the health, the provision, the safety, and everything that is good in your life, even if you do not see it in the physical realm; it is yours, bought and paid for in full by the sacrifice of Jesus. Let your requests begin and end with thanking Him.

Philippians 4:8 *Finally, brethren, whatsoever things are true, whatsoever things are honest, whatsoever things are just, whatsoever things are pure, whatsoever things are lovely, whatsoever things are of good report; if there be any virtue, and if there be any praise, think on these things.*

Philippians 4:6 *Be careful for nothing; but in every thing by prayer and supplication with thanksgiving let your requests be made known unto God.*

Revelation 7:12 *Saying, Amen: Blessing, and glory, and wisdom, and thanksgiving, and honour, and power, and might, be unto our God for ever and ever. Amen.*

8. Confess God's healing.

You keep your healing by believing. "By His stripes I am healed and by His stripes I am kept healed." God tells you there is life and death in the power of your tongue. We begin by confessing what God says we have. We have health. Speak to the mountains and tell them they are perfectly healthy and whole. There is so much power in His Words. He spoke the Word and there was Life. When we speak a word, is it life? Or is it death? Speak life and things will go much greater for you.

Praise and worship also ushers in the power of God. Praise is power! What exactly is praise and worship? It is simply thanking this incredible, loving God for the completed finished work He did for us all. Paul and Silas began to worship and sing to the Lord and the chains dropped from them and they were released from prison. They were praising and worshiping before they saw with their eyes the finished work. Remember it was the miracle, the 'signs and wonders' that brought the jailer to salvation. (Acts 16)

Our days should be filled with praise and worship and prayer. We do not need to set a specific time or wait for church services. We can do it all day, everyday. I love the praise and worship time in my church, it is powerful when all his people come together to worship and praise Him. I love this time. I am so unworthy, that's what makes it so incredibly wonderful! My days are spent thanking God for His healing, my home, a praise report, a client delivered, I could go on. It's an all day event. I remember being laughed at when I first came to Jesus by those who had been serving Him for a long time. I thought I must have this relationship with My Jesus wrong, for here are people who say they have known Him for years and years and years and they are making fun of my relationship with Him. If anyone would mention a challenge I would simply either pray right there and thank God for His provision in the situation or just praise and thank Him by speaking to the mountain. This to me encompasses praise and worship, it is simple. "Thank you; thank you my Jesus, my God, Thank You." The more I know of Him the more I love Him and want to please Him.

Keep speaking about God's goodness.

Do this wherever you are. I know you cannot do it at your work place if you work in a secular job, not very loud anyway! But do it on your break, whisper it, speak it on your way to work and on your way home. Feed that belief in you. As your heart continues to flow in worship you will get stronger, spiritually and physically. This is one step in maintaining your health. (Giving no thought to the Enemy's lies.) It is hard to hear the Enemy's lies when you are praising and worshipping God, but Satan and the world will try to keep you from hearing. When you feel an ache or a pain, praise God. Don't give thought to the physical, except to take your authority over it and command it to leave.

Mark 5:19 ... *Go home to thy friends and tell them how great things the Lord hath done for thee, and hath had compassion on thee.*

KEEP building your belief.

By starving your unbelief and feeding your belief you will soon find yourself looking into the face of Jesus Christ when you look in the mirror. I want to be a reflection of Him, but if we still look like the world and act like the world and walk in unbelief, we will not have the likeness of Jesus.

Start by not reading all the stuff doctors write about. I think it must be very difficult for doctors and nurses to believe in the healing power of Jesus Christ and that we have it in us supernaturally. They set their minds on studying everything about man's healing ways, they are not taught about God's healing in medical school. (There may be a few that teach about the Lords healing). When they no longer can do anything to help someone, they might turn to God then for that healing, but they take years studying medicine and what man made things can help. I believe medicine and doctors are for the unbelievers. I thank Him for their gifted hands and education to heal the unbelievers. Yes, that was me at one time, I now know that I have the best physician, His name is Jesus. He took all our sickness at the cross, every disease, infirmity, mental torment that's out there and ever will be out there. We no longer have to suffer from any of these things because He took our infirmities and carried our diseases for us already. It is finished!

I turn off the TV, stop reading magazines, and only look at a few things in the newspaper. I separate myself from unbelieving people as much as possible who are willing to be used by an Enemy who comes to steal, and kill, and destroy. I stop hanging around losers, (Those who do not have Jesus and trust in doctors and lawyers only!) I know that sounds pretty radical. I am radical about my Jesus. I want it all, everything He has for me (for you) but I wasn't getting it by sitting under false teachings, listening to all the commercials about every sickness and disease and what pill was going to help this symptom. If you listen to the commercials on drugs, the side effects are worse than the original symptom they are trying to mask. Now I am not always the brightest person on earth, but I'd rather have a corn on my toe than be paralyzed for life or lose my entire foot from some drug that they said was going to help. (Just an analogy!) But you have heard these commercials if you watch TV at all. Certain programs aired have every commercial that is selling some kind of drug that is there to help with something! Thankfully there is some TV that I feel I can watch without having to mute every commercial, or continually talk back to the TV. I refuse to receive anything they just spouted. I know my husband thinks I am nuts at times, that's okay because I am nuts over my Lord. I love everything about Him. I didn't used to be able to say that before I heard the True Gospel of Jesus Christ. When I was living in the deception of the Enemy I had many things I thought that were the truth about our Lord, they were lies from the pit of hell. The Lord I know now I love everything about Him. I trust Him in everyway because of who He is, and what He did. He's not schizophrenic; He is not a hit a miss God. He doesn't pick and choose who gets healed, prospered or delivered today. He paid for it all 2000 years ago on the cross.

Ephesians 4:7 *Don't give place to the devil*

Romans 10:17 *Faith comes by hearing and hearing by the Word of God.*

James 4:7 *Submit yourselves therefore to God. Resist the devil, and he will flee from you.*

Partake of daily spiritual food by reading the word and studying God's word.

Hebrews 4:12 *For the word of God is quick, and powerful, and sharper than any two edged sword, piercing even to the dividing asunder of soul and spirit, and of the joints and marrow, and is a discerner of the thoughts and intents of the heart.*

1 Thessalonians 2:13 *For this cause also thank we God without ceasing, because, when ye received the word of God which ye heard of us, ye received it not as the word of men, but as it is in truth, the word of God, which effectually worketh also in you that believe.*

If we do not know the truth about what our Lord has provided for us, then we can perish in our lack of knowledge and understanding. Most people wait until they are in need of a miracle before looking to God for all the answers and before they begin to really study to show themselves approved, believing in His finished work. When we know the truth, it sets us free in every area of our lives. With those freedoms comes responsibility. When you feel the old symptoms of sickness trying to come upon you, speak to the mountain, remember it is Jesus who lives in you; it is by His authority that we have power to move mountains, if you believe. His name is filled with power and you have it inside you. Or just shout, "JESUS HELP!" that's always a pretty good prayer, or "Thank you Jesus."

Isaiah 33:24 *And the inhabitant shall not say, I am sick*:

Do not say, "I am sick." I know many of you have been taught as I had that this was like speaking a lie, because I felt sick, my physical body was sick. But to not say it, is wisdom from the King himself. Our words bring life. Saying I am sick is like speaking death. So you might say something like. I am having some challenges right now, but my God says "by His stripes I am healed" (2 Peter 2:24). Speak What God says I am.

Gratitude strengthens your relationship with Him and feeds your belief also. When I begin to thank Him for His incredible health for me and His love and provision, it is like Paul and Silas singing in prison before the doors opened. Gratitude opens the door for belief and action, the spoken word brings life.

John 15:3 *Now ye are clean through the word which I have spoken unto you.*

1 John 2:5 *But whoso keepeth his word, in him verily is the love of God perfected: hereby know we that we are in him.*

Keep on filling yourself up with the Spirit, the Spirit is life to all your flesh.

Hebrews 4:12 *For the word of God is quick, and powerful, and sharper than any two edged sword, piercing even to the dividing asunder of soul and spirit, and of the joints and marrow, and is a discerner of the thoughts and intents of the heart.*

Hebrews 13:15 *By him therefore let us offer the sacrifice of praise to God continually, that is, the fruit of our lips giving thanks to his name.*

Acts 6:4 *But we will give ourselves continually to prayer, and to the ministry of the word*

Psalm 71:14 *But I will hope continually, and will yet praise thee more and more.*

Make no room for the enemy. Be so filled with the Lord that there is no room at the inn for Satan's lies.

Mat 12: 43-45 *When the unclean spirit is gone out of a man, he walketh through dry places, seeking rest, and findeth none. Then he saith, I will return into my house from whence I came out; and when he is come, he findeth it empty, swept, and garnished. Then goeth he, and taketh with himself seven other spirits more wicked than himself, and they enter in and dwell there: and the last state of that man is worse than the first. Even so shall it be also unto this wicked generation*

God spoke to me about how when a person with addictions cleans their house and it is not filled with the Lord and His truths, the Enemy comes back in and brings seven more even stronger with him. This is why you see many alcoholics who have quit drinking for several years or months, if they begin to drink again, they are back at the place where they would have been had they never quit. Satan found that house empty and brought back those seven stronger to fill it because we did not fill it with the Lord and His truths. I think it's dangerous to help someone with an addiction and then not also help them to fill those empty places with God. It is just one more way to start digging that hole for their grave. I am guilty of this myself. I am not judging. It is our lack of understanding that allows us to do the many ignorant things we do in our lives.

Receive His grace, faith and love for you.

It is the faith of Jesus Christ that you have; you don't have to try to get more, pray for more or search for it. His Grace is what will sustain you and His love will pour out of you and spill out over those around you. Your heart will desire to give to others that which you have received by the faith of Jesus. You will want to share it to all who will listen. Your relationship with Him will not be a 'private matter' because you will so love Him that you can hardly contain yourself. His love should be a motivation to live Godly lives. Desire the more; you will never regret reaching out and taking hold of all that our Lord has for you and those around you. I have it, it's THE most wonderful thing I have experienced or ever will in this world. You will be so filled overflowing; spilling over, that others will want what you have. At the risk of looking foolish in the world's eyes and the risk of being rejected by a world who wants nothing to do with this incredible Jesus, grab hold of all He has for you. There will always be those who still want nothing to do with this incredible life in Christ. Though I still cannot understand that, except that they do not know the truth.

John 12:48 *He that rejecteth me, and receiveth not my words, hath one that judgeth him:*

Ephesians 3:19 *"And to know the love of Christ which passeth knowledge, that ye might be filled with all the fullness of God,"*

There is so much power and strength in the word of God. It fills me, encourages me and brings life.

I am sure I will receive criticism from those that don't believe, it won't be the first time. But I am not concerned. I am concerned with your life and if you are in need of a savior! If you have never given your life to Jesus Christ, Believe me it is not a boring life. It is filled with all the joy and peace, health and prosperity and this incredible love that is too wonderful to even explain. Your jouney has just begun. There is so much that God desires for you. Grab hold of and believe for everything He has provided through the sacrifice of His one and only Son, Jesus Christ

He is so worth it!

Prayer:
I desire wisdom more than gold, your love more than the world. Help me to want to read your word and have a passion to serve you. Help me to know your truth so that when the Enemy comes to steal the love and joy and healing I have, I can counter his lies with your word. I

love you Lord, thank you for your word." Thank you LORD that I am fearfully and wonderfully made, that I am loved unconditionally by you. Help me to know that there is nothing more for me to do but believe. That you sent your Son for me and it's a finished work, I have nothing to do. It's all about what you did. Thank you Lord for your finished work.

Amen.

Revelation 12:11 *And they overcame him by the blood of the Lamb, and by the word of their testimony; and they loved not their lives unto the death.*

Additional scripture references.

Mark 8:23 *And he took the blind man by the hand, and led him out of the town; and when he had spit on his eyes, and put his hands upon him, he asked him if he saw ought.*

Mark 8:22-26 *And he cometh to Bethsaida; and they bring a blind man unto him, and besought him to touch him. And he took the blind man by the hand, and led him out of the town; and when he had spit on his eyes, and put his hands upon him, he asked him if he saw ought. And he looked up, and said, I see men as trees, walking. After that he put his hands again upon his eyes, and made him look up: and he was restored, and saw every man clearly. And he sent him away to his house, saying, Neither go into the town, nor tell it to any in the town.*

2 Corinthians 5:17 *Therefore if any man be in Christ, he is a new creature: old things are passed away; behold, all things are become new.*

Luke 5:12-14 *And it came to pass, when he was in a certain city, behold a man full of leprosy: who seeing Jesus fell on his face, and besought him, saying, Lord, if thou wilt, thou canst make me clean. And he put forth his hand, and touched him, saying, I will: be thou clean. And immediately the leprosy departed from him. And he charged him to tell no man: but go, and show thyself to the priest, and offer for thy cleansing, according as Moses commanded, for a testimony unto them.*

Genesis 6:3 *And the Lord said, My spirit shall not always strive with man, for that he also is flesh: yet his days shall be an hundred and twenty years.*

Proverbs 20:27 *The spirit of man is the candle of the Lord, searching all the inward parts of the belly.*

1 Corinthians 2:11 *For what man knoweth the things of a man, save the spirit of man which is in him? even so the*

things of God knoweth no man, but the Spirit of God.

1 Corinthians 12:7 *But the manifestation of the Spirit is given to every man to profit withal.*
Acts 2:4 *And they were all filled with the Holy Ghost, and began to speak with other tongues, as the Spirit gave them utterance.*

2 Timothy 1:10 *But is now made manifest by the appearing of our Savior Jesus Christ, who hath abolished death, and hath brought life and immortality to light through the gospel:*

2 Corinthians 3:6 *Who also hath made us able ministers of the new testament; not of the letter, but of the spirit: for the letter killeth, but the spirit giveth life.*

Mark 4:24 *And he said unto them, Take heed what ye hear: with what measure ye mete, it shall be measured to you: and unto you that hear shall more be given.*

Philippians 1:27 *Only let your conversation be as it becometh the gospel of Christ: that whether I come and see you, or else be absent, I may hear of your affairs, that ye stand fast in one spirit, with one mind striving together for the faith of the gospel;*

1 Thessalonians 3:8 *For now we live, if ye stand fast in the Lord.*

Philippians 4:1 *Therefore, my brethren dearly beloved and longed for, my joy and crown, so stand fast in the Lord, my dearly beloved.*

GRACE

1 Corinthians 15:10 *But by the grace of God I am what I am: and his grace which was bestowed upon me was not in vain; but I laboured more abundantly than they all: yet not I, but the grace of God which was with me.*

Ephesians 3:8 *Unto me, who am less than the least of all saints, is this grace given, that I should preach among the Gentiles the unsearchable riches of Christ;*

Romans 15:15 *Nevertheless, brethren, I have written the more boldly unto you in some sort, as putting you in mind, because of the grace that is given to me of God,*

Psalms 84:11 *For the LORD God is a sun and shield: the LORD will give grace and glory: no good thing will he withhold from them that walk uprightly.*

LOVE

Revelation 1:5 *And from Jesus Christ, who is the faithful witness, and the first begotten of the dead, and the prince of the kings of the earth. Unto him that loved us, and washed us from our sins in his own blood,*

1 John 2:15 *Love not the world, neither the things that are in the world. If any man love the world, the love of the Father is not in him.*

1 John 3:1 *Behold, what manner of love the Father hath bestowed upon us, that we should be called the sons of God: therefore the world knoweth us not, because it knew him not.*

1 John 3:16 *Hereby perceive we the love of God, because he laid down his life for us: and we ought to lay down our lives for the brethren.*

1 John 4:10 *Herein is love, not that we loved God, but that he loved us, and sent his Son to be the propitiation for our sins.*

1 John 4:19 *We love him, because he first loved us.*

Galatians 2:20 *I am crucified with Christ: nevertheless I*

live; yet not I, but Christ liveth in me: and the life which I now live in the flesh I live by the faith of the Son of God, who loved me, and gave himself for me.

References:

www.cswmi.org - Connie Weiskopf Ministries
www.fathershousefc.com - Pastor Mike Miller
www.awmi.net - Andrew Wommack Ministries
www.josephprince.org - Joseph Prince Ministries
John G. Lake
Smith Wigglesworth – devotional

Made in the USA
Middletown, DE
09 February 2015